A Handbook in Intercultural Communication

Second Edition

JEAN BRICK

National Centre for English Language Teaching and Research
Macquarie University, Sydney NSW 2109

Published and distributed by the
National Centre for English Language Teaching and Research
Macquarie University
Sydney NSW 2109

Brick, Jean.

China : a handbook in intercultural communication.
2nd ed.

Bibliography.

ISBN 1 86408 910 5.

1. Cross-cultural orientation – Australia – Handbooks, manuals, etc. 2. Intercultural communication –
Australia – Handbooks, manuals, etc. 3. China – Social life and customs – 1976– . I. National Centre for
English Language Teaching and Research (Australia). II. Title. (Series : Language and culture series ; 1).

303.482

MACQUARIE
UNIVERSITY ∽SYDNEY

First edition printed 1991
Reprinted 1995, 1996
Second edition:
© Copyright Macquarie University 2004

The National Centre for English Language Teaching and Research (NCELTR) was established at
Macquarie University in 1988. The National Centre forms part of the Linguistics discipline
at Macquarie University.

Reviewed by Zhang Xinping, Hubai University, China
Project Manager: Louise Melov
Production Supervisor: Kris Clarke
Cover design first edition: Simon Leong
Book design first edition: Anna Soo
DTP second edition: Helen Lavery
Printer: Ligare Pty Ltd

ACKNOWLEDGMENTS

The first edition of this book would not have been written without the help and encouragement of a large number of people. I must thank Sue Benson whose extraordinary patience and enthusiasm guided me through many difficulties.

Professor Chris Candlin, Dr H Hendrischke and Kerry O'Sullivan made valuable suggestions on the manuscript. Professor Joe Mestenhauser and Dr Michael Page introduced me to cross-cultural training.

Above all, my thanks go to the Chinese who, through their friendship and understanding, introduced me to Chinese life and culture. To Mao Weilin in particular, and to Ye Zhou, Liu Zhengrong and Chen XiaoYun, I owe an enormous debt of gratitude.

In preparing the second edition of this book, my thanks go first of all to Louise Melov for her ongoing encouragement and editorial support. I would also like to thank Zhang Xinping of Asia-Australia Business College of Hohai University, whose careful, insightful and stimulating comments contributed enormously to this work. All responsibility for misunderstandings, however, remains my own.

For the pictorial material included in this second edition, I extend my thanks to Dr Paul Kotala, Louise Melov, Margaret Considine and Sky Garratt for the provision of their images of China.

Jean Brick

TABLE OF CONTENTS

CHAPTER ONE

INTRODUCTION

What is cross-cultural communication?

Once upon a time a marmoset decided to leave the forest and explore the great, wide world. He travelled to the city and saw many strange and wonderful things but finally he decided to return home. Back in the forest, his friends and relatives crowded round. 'Well,' they cried, 'what did you see?' 'I saw buildings made of concrete and glass. Buildings so high that they touched the sky,' said the marmoset. And all his friends and relatives imagined glass branches scratching the sky.

'The buildings were full of people walking on two legs and carrying briefcases,'said the marmoset. And his friends and relatives could almost see the people running along the branches with their tails wrapped firmly around their briefcases.

What is Australian about an Australian? Or Chinese about a Chinese? Or German about a German? If someone is described as a dinky-di Aussie, what does it mean?

In answering such a question, we would probably point to certain ideas, certain ways of behaving, perhaps certain products that would, in general, be associated with the concept of 'an Australian'. We would, in fact, describe a culture. Members of a particular culture have certain things in common, a certain way of life, a certain way of behaviour. What they share includes certain values and beliefs, certain customs, perhaps certain gestures or certain foods. They may also share distinctive artefacts, a distinctive art, a distinctive music and a body of literature and folk stories.

This way of regarding culture as observable patterns of behaviour is a useful one but one that has its limitations. One question that tends to remain unanswered is what leads members of a particular culture to agree that certain behaviours have certain meanings. For example, how does an Australian man know that when another man approaches him in a pub, slaps him on the back and says 'How ya goin' you ol' bastard', he is expressing friendship and intimacy?

Members of a culture share patterns of behaviour, but they also share models of how the world works and how its myriad aspects relate to each other. These models are crucial not only in deciding how to interpret what is going on in any given situation, but also in moulding actions and responses. In other words, culture can be seen as shared knowledge, what people need to know in order to act appropriately within a given culture.

However, it is also important to remember that a culture is not a static entity; it is constantly changing, constantly evolving under the impact of events and as a result of contact with other cultures. Changes in certain aspects of a culture, especially in the area of behaviours and customs, can occur rapidly. Changes in the underlying values, in ways of looking at the world, tend to be much slower.

Language and culture

As children grow up, they learn how to act within their culture. They learn what actions are appropriate in a given situation, and how to interpret the actions occurring around them. At the same time, they are learning to speak their first language. Language and culture are, of course, inextricably linked, so that learning language means learning culture and vice versa. For example, a child growing up in one of the English-speaking cultures learns to say 'Can I have a drink?' rather than 'Give me a drink'; she learns to address her brothers and sisters by their names regardless of whether they are older or younger than herself; she learns to say 'thank you' when accepting something. In other words, in learning how to speak, a child must not only master the vocabulary and grammar of a certain language, she must also absorb the social rules that govern how she should use her vocabulary and grammar in concrete situations. She absorbs a world view that relates these various situations together into a meaningful whole. She learns a culture that is largely, though by no means totally, expressed through language.

However, this world view is generally not a consciously reached, consciously held world view. Just as people are often unable to describe – even on a simple level – the grammatical rules of the language they speak, so they are equally unconscious that their habit of addressing siblings by their given name (and even having a given name and a family name) arises from a way of looking at the world that has been learned, and that other people from other cultures may have other world views that do not necessarily share this way of addressing siblings.

This becomes important when we realise that in moving from one culture to another, people take their world view with them. It informs their interpretation of the new situations they experience, so that the interpretations they reach are frequently inappropriate. Like the marmosets, they see the world through the spectacles of their own culture. The interpretations they put on events in the new culture frequently do not match the interpretations reached by members of this culture. An example illustrates the possible consequences:

When the first Vietnamese refugees began to arrive in Australia in 1978, many of them settled in Cabramatta, a south-western suburb of Sydney. At that time, the majority of the shops in Cabramatta were operated by Australians or by migrants who had lived in Australia for a considerable period and who had to a great extent acculturated, at least in regard to behaviour accepted in service encounters in shops. When a Vietnamese went into a shop, he would ask for what he wanted: 'Give me a packet of cigarettes', 'I want a kilo of pork'. In Vietnamese, the direct translation of their words was totally appropriate. However, the Australian shopkeeper concluded from the lack of softeners, 'Could I have …', 'Have you got …', and from the lack of 'please' and 'thank you', that the Vietnamese was rude. He therefore raised his voice slightly and spoke a little more abruptly. The Vietnamese, observing this, concluded that, as he himself had behaved perfectly normally, the reason for this very obvious display of anger must be racism. He therefore used body language to convey his contempt for the shopkeeper … and so on. In the end, the majority of shopkeepers were convinced that Vietnamese were arrogant and impolite, while the majority of

Vietnamese were equally convinced that the shopkeepers were arrogant, impolite and racist to boot.

This type of mutually reinforcing mistaken interpretation is something that happens continually in cross-cultural encounters as each participant is guided in both his interpretation and his action and reaction by a world view that is largely responsible for determining what should be said, where and in what way.

Culture and language teaching

With language and culture so inextricably linked, it is obvious that a language learner has more to do than master a new grammar and vocabulary. She must also learn what utterances are appropriate to particular situations. To state this is to state one of the fundamental principles of modern language teaching. Very few teachers would disagree that the language being taught needs to be presented in contexts mirroring as far as possible the contexts in which it occurs in everyday life. Furthermore, the language taught must be appropriate to those contexts. However, many teachers tend to be unaware of the extent to which the considerations determining appropriateness are not shared by students from different cultural backgrounds. For example, when teaching a function such as 'asking for permission', many teachers assume that once modals have been presented and practised in a specific situation, then the student should have no further trouble in asking his employer for a day off work. However, the function 'asking for permission' involves not only a form of words but also a mental construct that determines when it is appropriate to actually ask, what reasons, if any, it is appropriate to advance, and how directly or indirectly permission should be sought.

Even when teachers are aware of differences in mental constructs, this does not always usefully reflect itself in classroom practice. Most teachers are aware that differences in topic selection on first meeting may result in their Chinese students asking people's ages. They therefore warn students against this. However, by vetoing this and a number of other questions commonly asked by Chinese on first meetings, teachers effectively leave their students with nothing to say. In other words, teachers tend to teach what not to say, but not what to say.

Teaching culture

This book is aimed at helping integrate culture learning into the language learning process. It starts from the premise that any attempt to examine cultural issues must be on the basis of mutual exploration.

We have already seen that cultural rules tend to be unconscious, that they are acted upon rather than thought about. This means that both teachers and students may be largely unconscious of the considerations of appropriateness that govern their speech. Thus the Chinese student finds it natural to address his teacher as 'Teacher Mary' while the Australian teacher finds it equally natural to be addressed as 'Mary'. In order to successfully integrate considerations of cultural appropriateness into language teaching, it is necessary that both teacher and students examine their own assumptions of what is natural. This mutual exploration, and the establishment of the relativity of what is considered to be natural, allows participants from both cultures to be both teachers and learners.

Having each participant in the classroom fill both teacher and learner roles has several consequences. Most importantly, it places each culture on an equal footing. If roles are not shared it is very easy, in examining cultural differences, for judgmental attitudes to appear. 'We do it this way' when coming from a teacher to students who have no opportunity of saying '... and we do it this way', may very easily be transformed into 'and so you should do it this way because it is right'. In dealing with cultural assumptions and cultural differences, value judgments need to be constantly guarded against.

If teacher and students are together examining their own cultural assumptions, the danger that a culture will be reduced to a list of dos and don'ts is also minimised. This is because both students and teacher are in a position to give an insider's view of one culture. An insider's view will inevitably be richer than that of an uninformed outsider and this should largely prevent any participant in the class from approaching the other culture as if it consisted of a series of permissives and prohibitions.

In integrating culture into the language classroom, we need to recognise that the aim is not so much to 'teach' culture as to teach cross-cultural communication skills. It is not possible, within the confines of the classroom, to expose students to the full range of a culture. Nor is it possible to prepare students for all situations in which differing cultural assumptions may cause miscommunication. It is, however, possible to develop in both teacher and student an ability to identify areas of possible misunderstanding so as to avoid such miscommunication. It is also possible to develop skills allowing participants in a situation to recognise when miscommunication has occurred, to analyse its probable cause and therefore to attempt repair.

The major skills involved are the ability to suspend judgment, to analyse a situation as a native of that culture would analyse it, and to choose a course of action that is most culturally appropriate to the situation.

The ability to suspend judgment, to be tolerant, is necessary for anyone hoping to avoid miscommunication. It involves the learner recognising that every culture has its own logic and its own integrity, and that no one culture is any better (or, for that matter, any worse) than any other. This does not mean that the individual is forced into a cultural relativism that prevents him ever making any judgments. The point is that when judgments are made they are made in full recognition of their cultural relativity, and that the alternative point of view is also seen to have logic and validity.

In order to appreciate this logic, it is necessary to have some understanding of how a situation appears to a native of the culture in question. This in turn involves some knowledge not only of the customs and behaviours associated with the culture, but also some understanding of the world view, and the values and beliefs that inform those customs and behaviours.

Taken together, tolerance and an understanding of the major cultural assumptions of all participants in a cross-cultural interaction allow the possibility of choice in cross-cultural encounters. That is, situations can be managed or resolved according to the cultural rules most appropriate to the individual situation.

About this book

The approach adopted in this book involves investigating, in a rather abbreviated form, aspects of Chinese behaviour, Chinese experience and Chinese values and beliefs. The aspects chosen are those that relate to the aspects of Australian language and culture commonly encountered in survival and general English courses. After discussion of the Chinese situation, tasks for Australian teachers are designed to help them analyse their own assumptions and their own reactions to situations involving cultural differences. These tasks are followed by classroom tasks which are designed to help students explore both their own and Australian cultural assumptions.

Of the task types used, the majority should be familiar, but two perhaps need some introduction. These are the case study and the survey/small-scale research project. The case study describes an authentic example of miscommunication and asks students to analyse what caused the miscommunication. They may also be asked to offer advice for dealing with the situation. There is no 'answer' provided to these case studies. It is expected that the teacher will contribute to the discussion and that the class as a whole will arrive at interpretations that are generally accepted by all.

Surveys and small-scale research projects involve observation of common Australian and Chinese behaviour. They aim to train students to observe and interpret the situations in which they find themselves; in other words, to enhance their independent learning skills.

Many of the exercises included as teachers' exercises can, in fact, also be used in the classroom; and conversely, exercises designed for classroom use can also be used by teachers interested in increasing their cross-cultural awareness.

Culture and the individual

This book deals in generalities. It talks about 'Chinese' and about 'Australians', each as a group with certain ideas and behaviours in common. The dangers of stereotyping and of overgeneralisation involved in this approach are very real. It is necessary to keep in mind that every person is both a member of a particular culture and at the same time an individual in his or her own right. Every person interprets the culture of the group to which he or she belongs in their own particular way. The extent to which the individual conforms to the patterns of his or her own culture, and the ways in which he or she expresses them, vary from individual to individual.

Differences in class, age, sex and geographical area, to name only some variables, will affect the expression and interpretation of cultural values. No one person is the embodiment of the 'average Chinese' or the 'average Australian'.

At the same time, it is important to define just what Australian and Chinese mean in relation to culture in this book. By 'Australian culture' I mean the total of those behaviours and customs, values and beliefs, and ways of interpreting the world that guide the interactions of the majority of Australian residents with other Australian residents.

These behaviours, values and beliefs have an Anglo-Celtic basis but have been modified by Australian residents in response to local conditions and as a result of contact with non Anglo-Celtic cultural groups which have also migrated to Australia. An

Australian is therefore someone who, regardless of ethnic background or place of birth, is socialised in these behaviours, values and beliefs and is able to use them appropriately in both determining his own actions and interpreting the actions of others. Such a person may of course also be socialised in an alternative culture or cultures but this does not mean that he is not an Australian. Such a person has two (or more) cultural identities.

A similar definition applies to Chinese culture. In this case, the descriptions in this book are based on the behaviours, values and beliefs and the ways of interpreting the world that are regarded as appropriate by city dwellers in the People's Republic of China. While some of the descriptions in this book are applicable also to residents of Hong Kong and Taiwan, it is important to remember that previously existing regional variations and vastly different histories during the past 40 years have resulted in significant cultural differences.

Attitudes to culture

The preceding discussion focuses on what is shared by way of behaviours, beliefs, customs and interpretations as a means of defining members of a particular culture. It is a definition that implies a measure of choice regarding cultural identity. A person can, for example, at least theoretically learn to be an Australian by adopting Australian behaviours, customs and beliefs.

This way of approaching culture may not necessarily be shared by Chinese students, many of whom may believe that being ethnically Han Chinese is a necessary part of being Chinese and belonging to Chinese culture. The results of this difference in outlook can be baldly summed up like this: Australians tend to believe that people everywhere are basically Australian. Cultural differences are seen as superficial and that, underneath, people really behave and believe as Australians do. Newcomers are therefore expected to speak English and are expected to conform to the Australian way of life. Failure to do so can be taken as evidence of hostility.

Most Chinese, on the other hand, tend to believe that a non-Chinese is different from a Chinese in a way that is almost impossible to overcome. This means, for example, that many mainland Chinese would accuse a person of Chinese ancestry whose behaviour does not reflect Chinese cultural norms, of 'forgetting the ancestors'. This is a serious charge, such people being regarded as little short of traitors. It is this feeling that underlies the anger that many mainlanders direct at supporters of Taiwanese independence. With regard to non-Chinese, it means that people are surprised when a non-Chinese speaks fluent Chinese or when he/she expresses an appreciation for something felt to be typically Chinese. Such appreciation may be interpreted as an unusual display of friendship or solidarity while a lack of adaptation is more to be expected and not necessarily indicative of hostility.

On the part of Chinese students, this may result in a ready acceptance of the existence of cultural differences and a willingness to explore them. At the same time, however, it may result in a belief that 'difference' is understood by Australians as a legitimate excuse for behaviour that does not conform to Australian expectations. 'Australians should understand us' is a commonly voiced opinion, and when it is found that

Australians do not necessarily either understand or accept cultural difference as an explanation, they may feel that Australians are being unreasonable. The general acceptance of the existence of cultural differences may actually hinder the acquisition of competence in handling instances of cross-cultural miscommunication. This is because Australians may be perceived as having a duty to understand, and such a perception may weaken any feeling of need regarding the necessity of acting in what Australians consider to be a culturally appropriate manner.

The organisation of this book

As this book is primarily aimed at teachers of English as a Second Language, it is assumed that students will actually be in Australia while they are studying English. In this case, many of them will be affected to a greater or lesser degree by culture shock. What culture shock is, how it manifests itself, and suggestions on how to cope with it are discussed in Chapter 2.

Chapter 3 aims at giving the teacher a brief introduction to the People's Republic of China, especially to its history, geography and economy. The second part of the chapter introduces some of the salient aspects of Mandarin (**Putonghua**), Mandarin being the official language of a country noted for its linguistic diversity. Brief introductions to the grammar and the writing systems are given, with the intention of noting major features only.

The description of aspects of Chinese culture begins with the self; firstly examining the self as it is officially defined on forms and by officialdom. The rest of Chapter 4 looks at the ways in which the self relates to family, to friends and to members of the opposite sex.

Chapter 5 takes themes related to everyday life, such as employment, housing, and shopping among others, and describes the general situation with regard to each. The focus is on differences with the Australian situation and on problems that are likely to result from these differences.

Chapter 6 examines the Chinese background to many of the themes occurring in basic English language courses, and also looks at some of the functions that are taught in such courses. The emphasis here is not on how these functions are realised in English as opposed to Chinese, but on the assumptions that underlie and determine the realisation of these functions.

Chapter 7 examines attitudes and values that are crucial to an understanding of how the world appears through Chinese eyes. This is followed in Chapters 8 and 9 by explorations of how these concepts are realised in business and education.

CHAPTER ■ TWO

CULTURE SHOCK

What is culture shock?

When people move from one culture to another, they suddenly find that much of what they have learned about interpreting the actions of people around them is suddenly irrelevant. They find that the strategies they have used to influence people or events in certain ways are no longer effective, the assumptions that guided their understandings and reactions are no longer reliable. Even distinguishing between the significant and the insignificant in a given situation becomes difficult, if not impossible.

This sudden psychological transition from competent adult to ineffective child inevitably results in the serious erosion of people's feelings of self-worth. They experience feelings of disorientation, frustration and helplessness. In short, they experience culture shock.

Culture shock is the result of the removal of the familiar. Suddenly the individual is faced with the necessity of working, commuting, studying, eating, shopping, relaxing, even sleeping, in an unfamiliar environment organised according to unknown rules. In mild form, culture shock manifests itself in symptoms of fatigue, irritability and impatience. Being unable to interpret the situations in which they find themselves, people often believe they are being deliberately deceived or exploited by host-country nationals. They tend to perceive rudeness where none is intended. Their efficiency and flexibility is often impaired and both work and family suffer. Some people may respond by developing negative stereotypes of the host culture, by withdrawing as much as possible from contact with host-country nationals, by refusing to learn the language and by mixing exclusively with people of their own cultural background. In extreme cases, rejection may be so complete that the individual returns immediately to his/her own culture, regardless of the cost in social, economic or personal terms. Alternatively, people may retreat into their own private world, either mentally or physically.

Physical symptoms of culture shock may include headaches, stomach-aches, diarrhoea, constant fatigue, difficulty in sleeping or excessive sleep and a general feeling of malaise. Unfortunately, many doctors are unfamiliar with culture shock and attempt to treat the symptoms rather than the cause.

The important thing to recognise about culture shock is that it is universal. It is experienced to a greater or lesser degree by all those who move from one culture to another. Experiencing culture shock does not mean that an individual is inflexible or inadaptable. It does mean that recognition of its virtual inevitability can lead to the development of steps to reduce its impact. The ways in which people adapt to unfamiliar cultures and the steps that can be taken to accelerate this process and reduce the severity of culture shock will be discussed below.

Have you ever lived for an extended period of time, say six months or longer, in a culture that is not your own?

a. Which aspects of the experience did you find most pleasant and rewarding?
b. Which aspects of the foreign culture were most difficult to adapt to?
c. How did you cope with culture shock?

If you have not yourself experienced living in a foreign culture, talk to someone who has. Ask them the above questions.

If you are a teacher, to what extent do you think that your students are suffering from culture shock?

If your company has staff based overseas, to what extent do you think they are suffering from culture shock?

Have you noticed any behaviour that might be explained in terms of culture shock?

How far and in what ways do you think that a teacher can help students cope with culture shock?

How far and in what ways might a Head Office help an expatriate staff member cope with culture shock?

Experiencing culture shock

We have made the point that culture shock is universal and virtually inevitable. This is not to say that it takes the same form in each and every individual. What does appear to happen is that most people go through a similar sequence of stages but that both the intensity of the experience and the time taken to go through each phase vary enormously from individual to individual.

In general, people go through four stages in the process of adaptation. The first stage, which is often very short, is the stage of euphoria. Everything seems fascinating. To the Chinese student, for example, Sydney is a wonderland. The streets are so quiet and clean, the office blocks in the city centre so modern, so developed. Similarly, the Australian in Beijing delights in the bicycles and the bustle, the overwhelming sense of history and the survival of tradition.

This feeling gives way, more or less rapidly, to a sense of alienation. People don't react as they expected to react. The Australian goes into a shop and waits to be served while the shop assistants are unconcernedly chatting away in a corner. The Chinese finds that the buses run once an hour along unmarked routes and the trains are always late. To do even the simplest thing requires massive effort and host-country nationals seem intent on being unhelpful, even deliberately obstructive. Things appear to happen without rhyme or reason.

This state of affairs lasts for an indefinite period of time and it is at this stage that the symptoms of culture shock manifest themselves. Gradually, however, most people start to adapt to the new environment. They learn the basic ground rules that enable them to interpret some of the situations in which they find themselves and to act in appropriate ways in those situations. Incomprehensible behaviour slowly becomes more comprehensible and, as this happens, the sense of being able to in some way control events returns. The feeling of alienation gradually decreases.

Many people do not go beyond this stage. Their adjustment is sufficient to allow them to operate effectively within the new culture when necessary. While they remain in many senses outsiders, they can participate in the host culture to the extent necessary to accomplish everyday tasks and to feel confident in doing so. Such people may oscillate between feelings of alienation and periods of relatively successful adjustment.

There is, however, a fourth stage: the stage of acceptance, of acculturation. In this stage, people are able to operate appropriately, effectively and confidently in a wide range of situations within the host culture. They will have internalised many of the host culture's norms so that their own outlook will have been modified. In a given situation they will be able to choose which set of cultural norms would be most appropriate to use in analysing and responding to that situation. In other words, they will be the cultural equivalent of people who achieve native or near-native speaker fluency in a language. They will be bicultural.

> Does bilingualism imply biculturalism?
>
> Is it possible to be bicultural without achieving bilingualism?

The process of cross-cultural adjustment can be graphed as a modified U-curve. The first stage, at the top of the U, rapidly leads into the frustration of the second stage, represented by the downward stroke. The third stage begins at the bottom of the U and things gradually improve as the graph climbs. For many people, the oscillations encountered in this third stage represent the extent of their cultural adjustment. However, for some, the fourth stage is reached when the graph gradually flattens out at a level roughly equivalent to that at the beginning of the U. (See page 15.)

This process of cross-cultural adjustment is one that all who move from one culture to another for an extended period of time undergo. There are, however, major differences between individuals in the time taken to go through the process and in the severity of the experience, especially in the second stage.

Coping with culture shock

While it is impossible to avoid culture shock altogether, it is possible to hasten the process of adjustment, and to mitigate to some extent the severity of the experience. This can be done by adopting a questioning and accepting attitude.

Firstly, it is important to remember the universality of the adjustment experience. An individual going through cross-cultural adjustment should remember that they are not alone, nor even unusual, in their frustration. It is not the result of personal inadequacy but a normal response to the total loss of familiar cues guiding interpretation and action.

Secondly, and this is more difficult, remember that the host culture does have its own logic and its own reasons for doing things in a certain way. Rather than starting from a belief that people are acting irrationally, that they are unfriendly and obstructive, it is more useful to start from the assumption that, in fact, people have valid reasons for acting as they do, even if those reasons are not immediately obvious. The task then is to discover what those reasons are. This is the first step on the road to cross-cultural sensitivity.

In trying to come to terms with the host culture, one of the most important resources for newcomers is people from a similar cultural background who have already been through the experience of adjustment. Such people will have lived in the host culture for an extended period and can provide valuable insights into the way it operates. At the same time, their own experience of the adjustment process can reassure newcomers that their feelings of alienation are not unique and that adjustment is possible.

Members of the host culture itself are also important. Newcomers should be prepared to ask questions about anything that they do not understand. People in general tend to enjoy explaining aspects of their own culture to others. However, it is important to phrase questions well. Rather than raising issues in a critical way, newcomers are likely to find that they get a better response if they raise problems or criticisms in a non-threatening manner. For example, in trying to understand the behaviour of an apparently rude shop assistant, they should attempt to describe the whole situation, including their own behaviour and the behaviour of the shop assistant and then ask for comments from the host national.

Two extremes need to be avoided. The first is to mix exclusively with people from a similar cultural background and to avoid contact with members of the host culture as far as possible. This strategy tends to prolong feelings of alienation because it limits opportunities to explore the host culture. Newcomers should seek opportunities to mix with host-country nationals and, difficult as this may be in a society like Australia, there are such opportunities. The major one is provided at work. Newcomers should make a conscious effort to participate in the informal groups that form at morning tea and lunch times. This participation may at first be passive, but as the situation becomes more familiar (and confidence in language use grows), participation can gradually become more active. Students will find similar opportunities before lectures and tutorials.

At the same time, newcomers can join groups which will allow them to interact with host-country nationals; religious groups, sports groups and international clubs are three obvious examples.

The second extreme to be avoided is the attempt to integrate totally and rapidly into the host culture, avoiding all contact with people of the same cultural background. Adapting to a new culture is an exhausting process. The individual needs to retreat to a familiar environment from time to time so as to be able to relax and let off steam.

Developing an investigative and experimental attitude towards the host culture can help speed the adaptation process. Newcomers should spend time analysing their interactions with host nationals. By trying to work out why people behave in a certain way, and by comparing notes with others in similar situations, newcomers can start formulating hypotheses about appropriate action that can then be tried out in situations in the future. So when newcomers know in advance that they will be involved in a certain type of situation they can formulate a plan of action based on their previous deductions and then monitor host nationals' reactions to it. Further modifications will undoubtedly follow as the newcomer learns more and more about the new culture.

Reading background literature on the new country, its history and geography, its system of government and its economy, helps to build a total picture of the culture. Reading some of the valued works of literature, in translation if necessary, watching films and attending festivals and other such public events are all important in creating a rounded picture of a culture.

Most importantly, newcomers should remember that relief will come, that they will not always feel frustrated, angry and alone, that others have been through the same experience and survived, and that the rewards to be gained in terms of broader horizons and a greatly enhanced understanding of both self and humankind make the whole process worthwhile.

If you are a teacher:

a. To what extent should the issues of culture shock and cross-cultural adjustment be addressed in language classrooms?

b. How would you integrate the consideration of such issues into the syllabus?

c. To what extent do you think culture shock is an issue for personnel transferred to Australia? How might you assist such personnel to cope?

If you are a human resources manager or businessperson:

a. To what extent should the issues of culture shock and crosscultural adjustment be addressed in preparing staff for overseas assignment?

b. How would you integrate the consideration of such issues into such preparation?

Classroom Tasks

■ TASK 1 ■

Do you think that your attitude to Australia and Australians has changed since you arrived here?

a. Think back to the time you arrived in Australia.
   ■ How did you feel?
   ■ What were your first impressions?

Compare what you remember about your first week with what other students in the class remember.

b. After one month in Australia:

- How did you feel?
- Had your impressions of Australia changed?
- What were the major problems that you encountered?

What about now?

- Do you feel the same now as you did after one month?
- How have your impressions of Australia changed over the time you have been in Australia?
- What are the major problems that you face now? How do they compare with the problems that you initially encountered?

■ TASK 2 ■

Has your teacher lived in a foreign country for more than six months?

With a partner, write down ten questions to ask about their experiences and about how they felt.

After they have answered your questions, compare their answers with your own experiences.

a. At the beginning of their stay, did they have similar feelings to you when you arrived in Australia?

b. What did they find most difficult in the new society?

c. How did they cope with differences in ways of behaving and thinking?

What can you learn from their experiences?

■ TASK 3 ■

What is culture shock?

With a partner, write down a definition of culture shock, then read the following article.

When you have read the article, look again at your definition. How would you modify it in the light of the article?

Culture shock

Culture shock is the name used to describe the feelings and behaviours of people who move from one cultural environment to another. This usually means that a person has moved from one country to another but it also applies to moves between different cultural regions within one country. In such moves, people find they have to cope with situations that are unfamiliar to them. They find that the ways of thinking and of behaving in the new culture are totally different from the ways that they are used to using. Everything, even the simplest thing, suddenly becomes difficult. Everything involves a lot of effort. At the same time, people in the new culture often seem to be deliberately unhelpful and to act without reason.

In reacting to this unfamiliar situation, people experience culture shock. They feel disorientated and frustrated. They are easily irritated and often develop negative feelings towards people from the new culture. For example, they may begin to feel that such people are cheating them. They feel hopeless and helpless, their efficiency declines and both work and family life suffer.

Physical symptoms of culture shock include headaches and stomach-aches, diarrhoea, fatigue, problems with sleep and general feelings of discomfort.

Culture shock is experienced by almost everyone who moves from one cultural environment to another, though its intensity varies from person to person. However, as people gradually adjust to their new environment its effects begin to lessen. The time taken for this to happen also varies from individual to individual, but once people realise that what they are experiencing is a common and temporary phenomenon they usually find that they can cope better with the symptoms.

Have you suffered any of the symptoms of culture shock?

What might you do to reduce the severity of culture shock?

■ TASK 4 ■

The graph below represents the different stages of culture shock.

Where do you think you are on the graph?

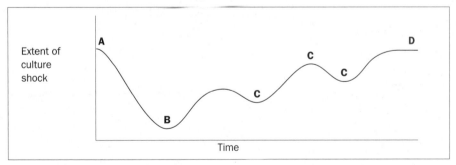

Key

A: Euphoria

I am very happy to be here. It's a wonderful place. Everything is interesting. This is the beginning of my new life.

B: **Depression**

Even the simplest things seem difficult. People here are lazy and often act in ways that I can't understand. I feel frustrated and hopeless. I don't feel well. My new life is terrible. Why did I leave home?

C: **Adjustment**

This country is not too bad. I'm beginning to understand some of their customs. The people are quite nice. I can make a new life here.

D: **Acceptance**

I feel very comfortable here. I understand the people and their way of life. Sometimes I act according to the new ways and sometimes according to the old. I have made a good life.

Discuss your answer with a partner. Are you both at similar stages or at different stages?

Can you give each other any advice for dealing with difficulties?

CHAPTER THREE

BACKGROUND
The People's Republic of China

The People's Republic of China is not a homogenous country. Geographically, economically and linguistically it is as divided as Europe. However, the existence of a common historical and cultural tradition has tended to reduce the significance of these differences, especially when viewing the country from outside.

History

The Imperial past

Chinese civilisation took root in the valley of the Yellow River during the second millennium BCE. Later history depicts this period and that which followed, up to about the middle of the first millennium BCE as, in the main, a kind of 'golden age'. As the Greeks looked back to the world portrayed by Homer for inspiration, later thinkers regarded the Shang and Zhou periods as representing an ideal to which they could only aspire.

During the following period, there developed dozens of independent states which gradually, from the fifth century BCE, conquered each other until by the third century BCE only seven states remained. These seven states were unified in 221 BCE by Qin Shi Huang, the first emperor and China's great unifier, better known in the West for the imposing array of terracotta warriors that accompanied him to his tomb. It was also in this period from the fifth century to the third century BCE that the basis of Chinese philosophy was established by figures such as Confucius and Mencius, to name only the most well known.

Qin Shi Huang's death was followed by a brief period of chaos before the founding of the Han dynasty (206 BCE – 220 CE). Under the Han, a great empire was built which, at its height, even had commercial dealings with faraway Rome.

With the collapse of the Han Dynasty at the end of the second century CE China broke into three kingdoms. This period provides the background for one of China's most loved novels, *Romance of the three kingdoms*, by Luo Guanzhong, which to this day forms the basis of innumerable operas, plays, novels and films.

China remained divided for more than 350 years, during the greater part of which the northern part of the country was ruled by non-Chinese dynasties drawn from the nomadic tribes inhabiting the areas north of the Great Wall. The country was reunified under the short-lived Sui Dynasty (580 – 618), which rapidly gave way to the Tang.

The Tang Dynasty (618 – 906) represented the culmination of China's early civilisation. Its capital, Chang An (modern Xian), was the greatest city of its time, a cosmopolitan trading centre that dominated an empire stretching from Central Asia to the Yellow Sea, from the steppes of Mongolia to Hanoi. The arts flourished and poetry in particular reached perhaps its highest peak. The examination system as the preferred method of recruitment for government office also gained importance during this period.

When the dynasty collapsed in 906 CE after an extended period of disorder, it was, in a familiar pattern, replaced by a number of feuding states. This time, however, the period of disunity was comparatively short and in 960 CE the Song Dynasty (960 – 1280) was established. The Song Dynasty was in many ways a watershed in the history of China. The examination system became virtually the sole method of recruitment to government office, and this led to the emergence of a bureaucracy that ruled the empire by virtue of its mastery of a literary tradition stretching back almost 1500 years. At the same time, a spectacular technical revolution that included more efficient methods of rice production, the invention of large sea-going junks and the introduction of paper money resulted in rapid urbanisation and the emergence of a society that was in many respects pre-capitalist.

This brilliant society collapsed in the face of the Mongol conquest, which put Kublai Khan, grandson of Genghis, on the throne as the first emperor of the Yuan Dynasty (1280 – 1368). In fact, vast areas of northern China had, since the middle of the 12th century, been under the control of two successive non-Han dynasties; the Mongol conquest, however, represented the first time that the whole of China had come under foreign domination.

This domination proved short-lived. Less than 100 years after the dynasty was founded, a rebellion engulfing the whole country overthrew the Yuan and established the Ming (1368 – 1644). As a native dynasty that came to power by defeating foreign invaders, the Ming sought to emphasise its continuity with the Song. However, the Ming emperors were autocrats to a degree undreamt of by the Song, and the attempt to marry the autocratic power of the emperor with the civil power of an examination-recruited bureaucracy resulted in catastrophe. From the end of the 16th century peasant rebellions occurred more and more frequently until, in 1644, the Manchu were able to use the fall of Beijing to a peasant army as an excuse for invasion.

The Manchu were a Tungus tribe from Manchuria and the dynasty they established, the Qing (1644 – 1911), was to be China's last imperial dynasty. By the mid-18th century the dynasty had created an empire unprecedented in its size and prosperity, an empire that dazzled European travellers and inspired such figures of the European Enlightenment as Voltaire and Leibnitz. Within a century, however, population pressure and economic recession triggered a series of peasant revolts, culminating in the Taiping rebellion that brought the country to its knees. Preoccupied with such internal problems and unused to dealing with foreign powers whose cultural and technical level approached or surpassed their own, the Qing did not at first appreciate the threat posed by European traders, who arrived in ever-increasing numbers from the beginning of the 19th century. Two Opium Wars forced the Qing to open many coastal ports to foreign trade and allowed foreign traders access to the interior. During the second half of the 19th century, as the power of the dynasty declined, the European powers struggled to ensure their own positions in the dismemberment of China that was to come.

The Republican period

The Qing Dynasty was overthrown in 1911, but, again in a time-honoured tradition, the overthrow was not immediately followed by the establishment of a new government. China was once again divided as various warlords competed for power. However, during the latter half of the 19th century, internal crises and the impact of western influence had dealt a death blow to the traditional bureaucracy, its ideology and its method of recruitment. New social forces were emerging that would radically transform the face of China. Most important was the development of a commercial middle class based in the great ports, particularly Shanghai. At the same time, middle-school and university students, faced with the loss of national independence, particularly in the face of Japanese aggression, were exploring new ideas from both the West and Japan. On 4 May 1919, in protest against a series of Japanese demands that would have resulted in the virtual loss of national sovereignty, these two forces came together in the May 4th Movement, which in many ways marked the beginning of the history of contemporary China. The enormous intellectual ferment that followed discredited the old learning and saw the development of many new schools of thought. The Communist Party was founded during this period.

By 1928 China was once again largely, though loosely, unified under Chiang Kaishek, who had assumed leadership of the nationalist party, the Guomindang, on the death of its founder Sun Yatsen in 1925. The Japanese were by this time increasing their presence and control, and in 1931 took over Manchuria, meeting little opposition in doing so.

The 1930s were dominated by two major developments. The Japanese constantly sought to increase control of Chinese territory, culminating in the declaration of war in 1937. At the same time, the Communist Party, having been driven out of its earliest rural base in southern China in 1934, completed the Long March and established another base in China's north-east. From 1936 it organised opposition to the Japanese invasion, at first in cooperation with the Guomindang, but increasingly in opposition. The defeat of the Japanese in 1945 was rapidly followed by full-scale civil war, which left the Communists in control of the whole country, barring Taiwan, in 1949.

China since 1949

The victory of the Communist Party was widely welcomed, not only by the peasants who formed the basis of its support but also by urban-based businesspeople and intellectuals who had despaired of Guomindang corruption. The early 1950s saw an enormous program of land reform that benefited the poorest sections of the peasantry, and the start of an ambitious program of industrialisation undertaken with the help of the Soviet Union.

In 1956 the Party officially called for criticism of its record and suggestions for the future. The vast outpouring of opposition that followed led to what proved to be only the first of a series of purges that culminated in the Cultural Revolution. Hundreds of thousands of people, both workers and intellectuals, were arrested and sent to forced-labour camps throughout the country.

That year, 1956, proved to be a prelude to the years of crisis: 1957–62. In an effort to pass rapidly to socialism, the collectives that had been established with land reform were converted into 26 000 communes. At the same time, efforts were made to industrialise the countryside, an endeavour symbolised by the backyard furnaces established all over the country to produce low-quality iron at great cost. The result of this policy, called the Great Leap Forward, was a famine which, according to the most conservative estimates, claimed ten million lives in 1960–61. At the same time, the Sino-Soviet split occurred, largely caused by differences over the process of de-Stalinisation in the Soviet Union.

By 1960 the disastrous nature of the Great Leap Forward had been recognised and several of its more extreme measures repealed. A small free market, for example, was once again permitted. These reforms were largely due to two leaders – Deng Xiaoping and Liu Shaoqi – who had effectively stripped Mao Zedong of substantive power. Mao, however, was not defeated and in 1966 reclaimed power under the auspices of the Cultural Revolution.

From one point of view, the Cultural Revolution merely represented a continuation to extremes of factional infighting at the highest levels of party leadership. At the same time, however, Mao managed to harness, for his own purposes, an immense feeling of frustration and discontent which had developed against the privileged party bureaucrats. The movement rapidly got out of hand and China came perilously near to civil war, with rival Red Guard factions fighting each other on the streets. In 1968 the army stepped in to take control and remained pre-eminent until the death of Lin Biao, leader of the armed forces and Mao's chosen successor, in 1971, allegedly as a result of an attempt to assassinate Mao himself. From that time until the death of Mao in 1976, the extreme-left Gang of Four, led by Mao's wife Jiang Qing, held power.

For the people of China, and particularly for intellectuals, the Cultural Revolution was an unmitigated catastrophe. Millions of people were arrested, imprisoned, beaten and sent into the countryside for re-education and hard labour. Schools and universities were closed and all vestiges of independent thought suppressed. Young people, two million from Shanghai alone, were sent down to the countryside to learn from the peasants. The economy came close to total collapse.

The death of Mao brought the Cultural Revolution to a close, as a group of party elders led by the twice-purged Deng Xiaoping moved quickly to arrest the Gang of Four and its supporters. Rapidly consolidating his power base, Deng inaugurated a policy of reform and opening up to the outside world that saw enormous changes during the 1980s. Economic growth was among the highest in the world, but brought many problems in its wake: unemployment, inflation and widespread corruption being three of the most serious. At the same time, exposure to the outside world highlighted China's relative backwardness and introduced new ideas that questioned the basis of the socialist system.

Anger at the extent of corruption and nepotism, fear of runaway inflation and unemployment, and tremendous uncertainty about the future all contributed to the protest movement of April–June 1989. This movement resulted in the emergence of the Elders, a group of eight largely retired senior party members, who stepped in and together with Deng and the more conservative members of the Central Committee forced the liberally inclined Party Secretary Zhao Ziyang from office. Shanghai Party Secretary Jiang Zemin was appointed in his place. The movement was bloodily repressed, not only in Beijing but also in the rest of the country, on 4 June 1989 and the following few days.

The next two years were marked by hardline attitudes on the enforcement of political and ideological orthodoxy and caution in relation to economic reform. The reform agenda was put back on track by Deng Xiaoping. In a much-reported tour of the south in January 1992 he repeatedly called for the pace of reform to be quickened. These calls were supported not only by leading reformers such as Li Ruihuan and Zhu Rongji but also by Jiang Zemin and his rival Li Peng, called the Butcher of Beijing because of his role in the Tiananmen massacre.

Fear of the growth of military influence, and specifically of the influence of Yang Shangkun, now state President and one of the Elders, and of his brother General Yang Baibing, resulted in both men being stripped of their responsibilities. This action strengthened the position of Jiang Zemin, who until then had had little independent control in spite of his ostensibly powerful position as Party Secretary.

Over the next few years, Jiang was able to slowly consolidate his position. He was helped in this not only because age gradually forced the Elders from the stage but also by a series of events that greatly weakened his opponents, notably Li Peng and the more reform-oriented Qiao Shi. Li Peng suffered from his association with Chen Xitong, the Mayor of Beijing. Chen was purged and imprisoned in a spectacular corruption case in 1995. Qiao Shi, chairman of the National People's Congress, was eased from power by the sudden imposition of an age limit of 70 on members of the Politburo Standing Committee in 1997. In addition, Deng Xiaoping, who had continued to exercise great power in spite of his retirement, died in February 1997. From 1997, Jiang Zemin exercised pre-eminent power.

Economically, the 1990s saw China on a roller-coaster ride to greater prosperity. After Deng Xiaoping's early 1992 tour of the south, the return to favour of economic reform resulted in an explosion of poorly regulated activity that led to a severe bout of inflation, reaching 17 per cent in 1995. This was followed by an equally severe deflation in 1996. From 1997, and particularly from 2000, however, the economy has been undergoing steady expansion. Reform of the huge, poorly performing and heavily subsidised state-owned sector accelerated from 1997. This has meant the closure of many factories and huge workforce reductions in others. However, official policy continues to favour the retention of state control over enterprises in key areas such as telecommunications, energy and banking. Policy also favours selling off smaller enterprises while attempting to reform larger ones. Privatisation has therefore had only partial success.

The same period has witnessed a phenomenal expansion in light industry, with China becoming the world's principle supplier of clothing and footwear. The vast majority of this growth has been centred in coastal regions, particularly in Guangzhou and Fujian in the south and in the Shanghai region. An estimated 100 million people from provinces in the interior have migrated to coastal regions seeking work in these new industries.

The flipside to this story of rapid development and the emergence of whole new industries has been a rapid increase in income inequality. Because much of the economic development of the 1990s was oriented to export markets, most new industry has been centred on the coast, to the detriment of the provinces of the interior. At the same time, reform of state-owned industries has hit hardest in the north-west, centre of the heavy industries that have born the brunt of reorganisation and closure. Millions of workers in this region have lost their jobs and many have been unable to find other work. According to World Bank figures, the Gini coefficient, which measures the extent of income inequality in an economy, has risen from 0.15 in 1978 to 0.40 in 2002. Peasant and worker dissatisfaction with this state of affairs has been expressed through unrest, including demonstrations, riots and strikes that are rarely reported in the western media. The need to reduce this level of inequality is a matter of increasing concern to the central leadership.

The generation of leaders which came to power after the Tiananmen massacre is known as the Third Generation. The First Generation was that of Mao Zedong, and was succeeded after Mao's death by the Second Generation, headed by Deng Xiaoping. The Party Congress held in November 2002 marked the handover of power to the Fourth Generation, headed by Hu Jintao. This is a significant transition, not least because it is the first time that power has been transferred peacefully and without major conflict. Leaders of the Fourth Generation tend to be more pragmatic and technologically oriented than their predecessors. All support the need to continue with economic reform, but there are differences of opinion regarding the role of the state in the reformed economy, with conservatives stressing the need for the state to retain a guiding role and reformers seeking a greater role for market forces. Reformers are also anxious to continue China's integration into the world economy, while conservatives tend to be wary of some of the effects of globalisation.

Several of the new leaders, including Hu Jintao and Premier Wen Jiabao, have spent many years early in their careers working in some of China's poorest and most backward regions. This has given these leaders an understanding of rural conditions that leaders of the Third Generation, whose experience was confined mainly to cities, did not have. Early actions of the new leadership demonstrate this concern, with a greater emphasis on the stimulation of consumer demand as an engine of growth and, of more immediate impact, the modification of the permit system which made it difficult for rural workers to legally move in search of work.

With regard to political reform, none of the leadership is likely to support the introduction of a multiparty democracy. This does not however infer that none would support the introduction or extension of elections for both party and lower level government positions. Within the Party some positions are already elected, and this is likely to expand. Some members of the Fourth Generation go further and advocate the extension of the elections, that are currently held at village level to select village leaders to township and ultimately to city and county levels. In all cases, what is envisaged is the presentation to the electorate of a list of candidates greater than the number of posts to be filled. Such candidates would not represent organised political parties.

Of the many challenges that face the new leadership, a number stand out. The first is the issue of unemployment and the growing gap between rich and poor, between city and country and between the coastal provinces and the provinces of the interior, that has been discussed earlier. The second is the problem of corruption. Corruption is widespread and includes the levying of a host of illegal fees and taxes on peasants by local authorities; the embezzlement of funds meant for community development, for flood control for example; the widespread use of bribes to gain exemptions from local regulations and favourable treatment in tendering processes and so on. It is regarded as a major problem because it relates directly to the popularity of the Party and of the government, as well as impacting on economic growth.

Pollution and environmental degradation are two more major problems. In spite of recent initiatives aimed at reducing air pollution caused by the burning of sulphur-rich coal, northern Chinese cities continue to experience some of the worst air pollution in the world. Poor agricultural practices have resulted in widespread degradation of agricultural land; and the wholesale clearing of forests, especially in the upper reaches of the Yangtze River, have contributed largely to severe annual flooding in central and southern China. The north of the country is also experiencing a critical shortage of water. The North China Plain is home to one third of the country's population but has only 7.5 per cent of natural water supplies. Much of the ground water is polluted as a result of unregulated industrial development. Ensuring adequate supplies of clean water for the population and for agriculture and industry will constitute a very real challenge in the next decade.

Health and education face major problems because each was starved of funding during the boom years of the 1990s when attention was focused elsewhere. In many rural areas, funds have not been available either to pay teachers or to maintain schools, and poorer peasants have been unable to afford to keep their children in school. Health services have also been dramatically run down, so that when the SARS epidemic hit in the first half of 2003 hospitals had great difficulty in coping. The culture of secrecy that attempts to deny or minimise bad news for fear of loss of social control exacerbates the difficulties of the health system in particular. The SARS crisis is a stark example of how unwillingness to communicate bad news can result in the rapid spread of a disease. HIV/AIDS is a further example. For many years Chinese health authorities refused to acknowledge the extent of HIV infection and even now inadequate attention is given to the need for preventative educational programs. As a result, the World Health Organisation has warned that China could have more HIV/AIDS infections than sub-Saharan Africa by the end of the first decade of this century. This has the potential to impact significantly on economic development.

In facing these challenges, the Fourth Generation of leaders is likely to experience the type of supervision and oversight from retired Third Generation leaders that Jiang Zemin experienced during his first few years in power. In addition, the inclusion in the leadership of people with a range of views on significant questions means that change is likely to continue at a fairly steady pace in the foreseeable future.

Geography

The People's Republic of China embraces an enormously diversified terrain. The country as a whole is extremely mountainous with rugged mountain chains separating the fertile river valleys in which civilisation developed. The two most important river systems are those of the Yellow River and the Yangtze River.

After rising in the far western province of Qinghai, the Yellow River loops north before flowing through the great plain of northern China, the cradle of Chinese civilisation. The Yangtze River also rises in Qinghai but flows south through Sichuan. As it leaves Sichuan it passes through a series of spectacular gorges which historically provided one of the few access routes into this isolated but fertile province. The lower Yangtze valley is in many respects the heartland of modern China, a rich rice-growing area which in recent years has also undergone immense industrial development.

The division of China by these two great river systems is reflected in a major agricultural division. North of the Yangtze River wheat is the dominant crop, while the Yangtze basin and the south are rice-growing areas.

A further division is represented by the open plain and steppes of Manchuria and Inner Mongolia to the north. Here the traditional agricultural pattern was nomadic pastoralism, a way of life that has largely disappeared, especially in Manchuria. The Manchurian plain was the earliest area of China to be industrialised and it remains one of the chief centres of heavy industry.

South-west China is extremely mountainous, culminating in the immense ranges of Tibet. North of Tibet the high plateau of Qinghai is separated from the open steppe of northern Xinjiang by the Taklamakan desert, a desert that lays justifiable claim to being the most inhospitable in the world.

Finally, mountain ranges crisscross the southern provinces of Fujian, Jiangsu, Guangdong and Guangxi, with the majority of the population living along the coastal plains and in the river valleys.

Excluding Taiwan, the country is divided into 30 provinces. The four great cities of Beijing, Shanghai, Tianjin and Chongqing form special administrative areas of their own.

Climate

China's climate is as varied as its terrain. The north is dry to arid with cold, clear winters and hot summers. Hot, humid summers and cold, wet winters are the pattern in the lower Yangtze delta, while the southern provinces have a monsoon-dominated tropical climate.

Economy

Twenty years ago, China's economy heavily depended on agriculture. The state-owned manufacturing sector was dominated by heavy industry, and was bedevilled by inefficiency, corruption, shortage of capital, outdated machinery, poor transport links and massive overstaffing. However, a small but dynamic private sector was developing in the shadow of state-owned enterprises, filling needs that the state sector lacked the responsiveness to recognise or meet.

At the beginning of the third millennium, this picture has changed dramatically. Agriculture now accounts for only 15 per cent of gross domestic product (GDP), industry and construction for 51 per cent and services for 34 per cent. Overall, state-owned enterprises account for only 37 per cent of GDP, and the huge increase in services has largely occurred in the private sector. However, agriculture continues to employ 50 per cent of the workforce, while industry employs 22 per cent and services 28 per cent.

Agriculture benefited greatly from the first round of reforms in the early 1980s. Since then, however, the government has sought to control food prices to the benefit of urban dwellers, with the result that the economic position of peasants declined during the 1990s. Millions of peasants have flocked to the cities to take up jobs in the new factories and to fill those positions that no one else wants, positions that are dirty, difficult and dangerous. The wholesale rebuilding of China's great cities, which proceeded at breakneck speed in the 1990s, would not have been possible without the labour of these people. With China's entry into the World Trade Organisation (WTO) the challenges to Chinese agriculture are likely to grow, as costs far outstrip international costs of production. Huge investment is needed to upgrade agricultural practices and to reverse the damage caused by poor techniques.

Reforms in the industrial sector have resulted in a reorientation from heavy industry to light industry, including clothing and footwear, electronics and white goods. This has been largely export driven, but some of the Fourth Generation leaders who assumed power at the beginning of 2003 have indicated that they may favour a greater focus on stimulating domestic demand. This move is aimed at improving the living conditions of peasants and reducing the gap between their living standards and those of city dwellers.

Of equal if not greater significance has been the emergence of the private sector, which now accounts for 33 per cent of GDP, compared with the state sector's 37 per cent. Much of this expansion has involved the service sector, which encompasses everything from small sidewalk restaurants to thriving accounting practices. The development of an urban middle class with high aspirations and some degree of disposable income has been an important consequence of this development.

Official Chinese figures state that the economy grew at steady 8 per cent per annum from 1997 to 2002. Some western economists doubt this, but most agree that this figure is likely to be correct for the years since 2000. The economy does, however, face significant problems, notably the issue on non-performing loans – that is, loans made to state-owned enterprises on political rather than economic grounds. These are so large as to pose a significant risk to on-going economic prosperity in the event of a major international down-turn. Another problem is the dependence of the economy on exports to only one market, that of the United States. Any significant economic downturn in the United States would have an immediate impact on China.

However, the entry of China into the WTO, while posing its own problems, signals China's desire to integrate into the international economic system and has the potential to facilitate further development by encouraging reform in areas such as law. There is no reason therefore to be pessimistic about the long-term prospects for the Chinese economy.

Ethnic groups

The vast majority of the population of China are ethnically Han, the name given to those whom Australians would normally refer to as Chinese. However, five per cent of the population belong to non-Han ethnic groups and the majority of these inhabit the strategically important, resource-rich and underpopulated border areas. Tibet is of course the most well known of these areas. To the north of Tibet, Xinjiang is home to several different ethnic groups of whom the Turkic Uighurs are the most numerous. Mongolians are concentrated in Inner Mongolia and the north-east. In the south-west the ethnic picture is remarkably complex, but the majority of non-Han peoples belong to various Thai groups.

All minority areas have seen enormous influxes of Han people, particularly since 1949, and in most cases the indigenous peoples are now vastly outnumbered. In Inner

Mongolia, for example, only about 5 per cent of people are Mongolian. In other areas, notably Tibet and Xinjiang, there is increasing opposition to Han incursions and Chinese rule.

In this book the focus is on the Han, who are referred to throughout as Chinese.

Languages and dialects

The linguistic map of China is a complex one. Apart from the languages of the more than 50 minorities that live in China, the Han Chinese themselves are divided linguistically into several dialect groups. The language of the north, of the capital, and therefore of the educated elite, is Mandarin. Mandarin, or *Putonghua*, the common language, is the official language of China and also the daily language of a significant proportion of the country, including the north-east, the provinces north of the Yangtze River, the north-west and the south-west. As the official language, it is the lingua franca of the educated elite and is widely understood in urban areas. However, in areas where other dialects are in daily use, Mandarin tends to be limited to formal settings. For example, the people of Shanghai speak Shanghai dialect with family and friends and also at work, reserving Mandarin for those occasions when non-Shanghainese are present, and for formal occasions. Even in the cities a significant number of older people and people with a lower level of education do not speak Mandarin or do not speak it well. In rural areas other than those where Mandarin is the local dialect, the majority of people do not speak Mandarin.

Apart from the north-east, the north-west and the south-west, the rest of the country is divided into seven major dialect areas, and each dialect is further divided into a number of varieties. Cantonese dialects are spoken in the southern province of Guangdong, which also has substantial numbers of Hakka speakers. The people of Shanghai speak a distinctive dialect, one of the Wu dialects, of which there are several varieties in the general Shanghai region. To the south, the people of Fujian speak two varieties of the Min dialect, while further south and west, Hakka dialects, already mentioned in relation to Guangdong, predominate. The people of Jiangsi speak one of the Gan dialects and the people of Hunan speak varieties of Xiang.

It is important to remember that these dialects are largely mutually unintelligible, and that, especially in areas such as the hinterlands of Shanghai and Guangdong, a few kilometres is sufficient to move from an area where one variety of a dialect predominates to an area where another variety is used.

In spite of this linguistic diversity, two factors maintain unity. The first is, of course, that Mandarin is the language of the educated elite across the country. The second is that in spite of differences in the spoken language, the written language is common to all dialects. Because the Chinese writing system is not phonetic, the same text can be read and understood by a speaker of Mandarin, of Cantonese, of Shanghai dialect and, in fact, of any dialect. This can be better understood by thinking about the English words 'cough', 'bough' and 'through'. Although 'ough' is used in each word, its pronunciation changes radically from word to word. Following is a sentence written in characters, with its pronunciation in three major dialects: Mandarin, Shanghai dialect and Cantonese.

我 是 中 国 人

Wo	shi	zhong	guo	ren	Mandarin (*Putonghua*)
Ala	xi	zhong	guo	nin	Shanghai dialect
Ngo	hai	zhong	yup	yen	Cantonese
I	be	China		person	English
		(literally: middle			
		country)			

When two people speaking different dialects meet, it is not uncommon to see them quickly tracing characters on the palms of their hands to ensure that their words are properly understood. Newspapers printed in Beijing can therefore be read by people who neither speak nor understand Mandarin.

About Mandarin (*Putonghua*)

Mandarin is a tonal language, which means that a change of pitch on a word changes its meaning. There are four tones:

ma: high level tone	'mother'
ma: high rising tone	'hemp'
ma: fall rising tone	'horse'
ma: falling tone	'curse'

In respect to tones, Mandarin is relatively simple compared to Cantonese or other southern dialects, which have seven or more tones.

Mandarin also uses relatively few morphemes so that there is a large number of homophones. To overcome this problem, the language has resorted to compounding. This means that many words are compounded of two or more words, as, for example, is the case in the English 'blackboard'.

Mandarin does not mark case or number. In order to make a distinction between 'chair' and 'chairs' it is necessary to add another word, such as 'some' or 'many'.

Verbs are not marked for agreement with nouns, nor are they marked for tense. This means that verbs are not marked according to the relation between the time of the event and the time of speaking. There are, however, several markers of aspect, that is, Mandarin makes distinctions between events that are seen as a whole (perfective – *le*), as having duration (imperfective – *zhe*), and as having been experienced (experiential – *guo*). These distinctions are made using particles which are placed after the verb and which cannot be used on their own.

The perfective particle (Per.) *le* can be used after a verb to indicate that the event in question is viewed as whole or completed:

| Women | zai | na li | zhu– | le | san | nian. |
| We | at | there | live | Per. | three | year. |

'We lived there for three years.'

However, it should be noted that *le* is not the equivalent of the past tense in English, as the following example shows:

Mingtian   wo   jiu   xie   wan –   le.
Tomorrow   I   then   write   finish   Per.
'I'll finish writing tomorrow.'

Zhe is used together with a sentence final particle (Intensifier) **ne** to indicate a continuous action (Imp.):

Wo   shuo –   zhe   hua   ne.
I   speak   Imp.   word   Intensifier
'I am speaking now.'

It also indicates which of two simultaneous actions is of lesser importance:

Wo   zuo –   zhe   kan   bao.
I   sit   Imp.   read   paper
'I am sitting down reading the newspaper.'

Guo is used after verbs to indicate that an action is being or has been experienced (Exp.):

Wo   kan   jian–   guo   nei   ge   ren.
I   look   see   Exp. that   classifier   person
'I have met that person.'

Mandarin also uses a series of particles that are placed at the end of sentences to convey meanings that in English are conveyed by very different methods. For example, *ma* placed at the end of a sentence converts the sentence into a question:

Ni   shi   xuesheng   ma?
You   be   student   Question
'Are you a student?'

Another particle, *ba*, is used to make a suggestion:

Women   zou   ba.
We   go   Suggestion
'Let's go!'

Ni   he   kafei   ba.
You   drink coffee   Suggestion
'How about some coffee?'

A third particle, *le*, has a multitude of functions, one of the principal ones of which is to indicate that something has changed:

Cong qian   wo bu kan   dianshi,   xianzai wo kan   dianshi   le.
From before I   not look television, now   I   look television Change
'I didn't use to watch television, but now I do.'

There are three other sentence final particles which function as a warning, as a softener and as a response to an expectation respectively.

Another important feature which distinguishes Mandarin from English relates to the difference between subject and topic. The topic of a sentence is what the sentence is about. In the following, for example, the subject is omitted:

Shu   xie –   wan   le.
Book   write   finish   Per.

'The book, (someone) has finished writing it.'

Shu, 'the book', functions as the topic of the sentence; that is, it states what the sentence is about. It is not, however, the subject.

A sentence can have both a topic and a subject, as the following example illustrates:

Nei   ben   shu   wo   yijing   kan –   wan le.
That   Classifier   book   I   already   read   finish

'I have already read that book.'

'That book' states what the sentence is about, while the subject is 'I'.

English, of course, also makes use of topic constructions, particularly in speaking:

'About that report, have you read it yet?'

These constructions are far less common, however, than in Mandarin. Also, as was seen in the first example, a sentence in Mandarin may omit the subject all together but this is seldom possible in English.

Mandarin makes use of a large variety of expressions drawn from classical literature. These expressions are composed of four characters, and the ability to use them appropriately indicates that the speaker is well educated. There are literally thousands of such expressions and, being drawn from literature, each has a story attached to it. It is impossible here to illustrate the depth and variety of these expressions; one example will have to suffice:

ke   zhou   qiu   jian
carve   boat   seek   sword

The story behind this saying is as follows. A man from the state of Chu was crossing a river when he dropped his sword into the water. He quickly carved a mark on the side of the boat in the exact spot that he dropped the sword so that he would easily be able to find it again. The expression refers to a person who takes measures without regard to the surrounding circumstances.

Because the use of such expressions indicates a well-educated person, some Chinese may attempt to use English proverbs and similes in the same way. The result tends to sound overelaborate and forced to Australian ears.

The writing system

The Chinese writing system is not an alphabetic system. Rather, it uses a large number of ideographs or characters, each character representing a morpheme. Obviously this means that there are thousands of characters. However, just as the total vocabulary of English contains far more words than the average (or even the highly educated) person is likely to use or know, so it is in Chinese. Basic literacy calls for a recognition of about 2000 characters. An educated person would have a reading vocabulary of about 6000 to 10 000 characters.

Each character represents a single morpheme. However, because of the compounding tendency mentioned above, this morpheme does not necessarily (or even usually) mean that a character represents a word. Many words are composed of two or more morphemes and written with two or more characters.

看　見　知　道

kan	–	jian	zhi	–	dao
look	–	see	know	–	tell
	'see'			'know'	

Each character is itself composed of several parts, just as an English word is written using a number of letters. Of these parts, approximately 225 have special significance as they are used to order words (in a dictionary, for example) as alphabetical order is used in English. Words are also further ordered by the number of strokes it takes to write them.

The word that translates as China, for example, is composed of two characters, the first of which is *zhong*, 'middle', the second *guo*, 'country':

中　国

zhong　　guo

Zhong is composed of two parts: a square, which represents a mouth, and a vertical line:

The vertical line in this character has a special significance. In a dictionary, this character would be listed under the vertical line just as the word 'central' would be listed under 'c' in English. *Guo* is composed of three parts: a mouth; a vertical line crossed by three horizontal lines, which by itself forms the character for king, *wang*; and a small dot, usually referred to as a drop of water:

口 + 王 + 丶 = 国

(There is no truth in the rumour that this character, which has the appearance of a king is inside a border with a small dot at his feet, gives an accurate pictorial representation of the relative powers of rulers and subjects in modern China!)

So characters are composed of parts just as English words are composed of letters. There are, however, rather more parts than there are letters.

While it is generally true that characters are not phonetic, so that it is not possible to guess how they are pronounced from their written form, many characters do in fact have a phonetic element. An example is the written form of *ma*, meaning 'horse'. By adding the character for 'woman' we get the word 'mother', which sounds the same as 'horse'. Adding two mouths to the horse produces the word meaning 'swear', also pronounced *ma*. Confusion is avoided by the fact that each of these words is pronounced in a different tone.

马　　妈　　骂

ma　　　ma　　　ma
horse　　mother　　curse

Reading and writing characters is therefore by no means as difficult as it is often reputed to be.

A high value is still placed on beautiful writing; calligraphy continues to be a highly regarded art form. However, for everyday use characters are written quickly and in modified, cursive form, just as happens with written English.

The characters used in the People's Republic of China include many simplified forms of traditional characters, the number of strokes used to write each character having been drastically reduced. This means that newspapers and books published in Hong Kong and Taiwan, which still use traditional characters, can initially cause difficulties for readers from the mainland.

Another reform has affected the direction of writing. Traditionally, Chinese is written in columns starting from the top right-hand side of the page. When written horizontally, the lines read from right to left. Books and newspapers are read from what an English speaker would regard as the back of the book. However, the People's Republic uses a writing system similar to that of English in that it reads horizontally from left to right.

Romanisation

Many systems have been devised to write Chinese using the Roman alphabet. The system used in the People's Republic of China has, since the 1970s, achieved widespread international acceptance. This system is called *hanyu pinyin*. All children on the mainland learn the system in primary school, but once they start learning how to write characters it is often forgotten. It is therefore not uncommon to find people who have difficulty in recognising and spelling their own names in *pinyin*. This is especially true of newcomers to Australia who are trying to find their names on a list.

The pronunciation of *pinyin* can pose some problems to English speakers, so a rough guide is given below. While not completely accurate, this guide will at least prevent you making appalling errors!

Initials		Vowels and Diphthongs	
Pinyin	Example	Pinyin	Example
b	bin	a	father
c	lets	e	us
ch	church	ai	like
d	dig	an	darn
f	fat	ang	long
g	gate	ao	now
h	hill	ei	eight
j	jug	en	analogy
k	kind	eng	sung
l	lend	i	eat
m	man	ia	Iago
n	name	ian	lien
p	pen	iang	i-ahng
q	chat	iao	yow
r	real	ie	yet
s	set	in	in
sh	share	ing	ring
t	top	iong	i-ong
w	way	o	saw
x	she	ong	oo-ng
y	yet	ou	home
z	seeds	u	too
zh	garage	ü	like German umlaut
		ua	wa
		uai	wife
		uan	uwan
		uang	uwang
		ui	way
		uo	ohwa

CHAPTER FOUR

DEFINING SELF IN SOCIETY

In this chapter, we are mainly concerned with how people refer to themselves and to others and how they relate to the social groups closest to them, their family and friends. First, we'll examine aspects of official identity – that is, the collection of facts that constitute a person in the eyes of officialdom: name, address, date of birth and so on. We'll then consider how people address each other, before going on to examine the family structure and the role of various people within the family. Finally we'll consider how a person relates to his or her friends, what is expected of friends, what leisure activities are popular, what people talk about and what they want to know about each other.

Official identity

Official identity is defined here as the information that a person is expected to supply to those in authority when filling out forms. The type of information required in China does not differ significantly from that required in Australia, but the way of presenting this information often differs from that prevalent in Australia.

First of all, it should be remembered that in China every adult has an identity document which, most importantly, specifies the bearer's place of residence. When people move from one place to another, they have to obtain permits from the police which allow them to work and to find accommodation. Until mid-2003 many people, and especially those who were leaving the countryside to find work in the cities, encountered considerable difficulty in obtaining such documents, but changes to the system after a series of particularly egregious abuses came to light should make obtaining valid residence permits easier in future.

Naming

In Chinese, the family name comes first, followed by the given names:

Wang Dahai

Li Meihua

Most family names are single syllable, but there are a small number of double-syllable family names – Ou Yang, for example. The actual number of family names is very small – so small that the colloquial term for 'everyman', the common people, is 'old one hundred names'. While this is an exaggeration, it's not much of one. Women do not change their family name when they marry.

Given names are chosen by parents at birth, but Chinese does not have a class of personal names as English does. Names are chosen for their meanings and often reflect the hopes that parents have for their children. Traditionally, names were taken from literature, or reflected parental hopes for wealth and success. Girls' names often reflected what were felt to be feminine qualities. Many children born after 1949, and especially during the 1950s and 1960s, were given names that reflected the ideological and political situation of the time:

Zhou Aihua   –   Zhou 'Love the Country'

Wu Xuejun   –   Wu 'Learn from the Army'

Li Tiegan   –   Li 'Iron and Steel'

Virtually all given names are written with either one or two characters, and names written with two characters cannot be divided; the given name functions as one name, not two.

Learners of English, especially beginners, may not recognise their names when they are written using *pinyin* romanisation.

Some learners adopt English names for use with English speakers. This can be done by putting the English given name first, followed by the full Chinese name – a system widely used in Hong Kong:

Jenny Wang Xiaohong

Michael Tang Weihai

Address

Chinese addresses are written in reverse order to those of English. A typical Chinese address would translate as follows:

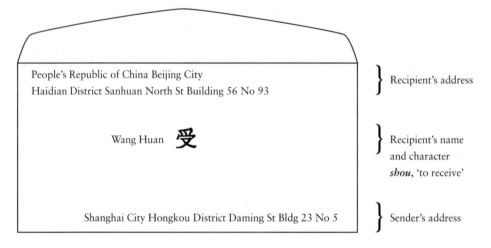

People's Republic of China Beijing City
Haidian District Sanhuan North St Building 56 No 93
} Recipient's address

Wang Huan 受
} Recipient's name and character *shou*, 'to receive'

Shanghai City Hongkou District Daming St Bldg 23 No 5
} Sender's address

The recipient's address is placed in the top left-hand corner, while the name is placed in the centre of the envelope followed by the character *shou*, which means 'to receive'. The sender's address is placed in the lower right hand corner. The sender's name is not usually included, because of the reluctance to expose names to strangers. (See Chapter 6, page 83.) Note the lack of punctuation and the use of the words 'city' and 'district'. Also, the building number comes before the flat number. Many Chinese who have just arrived in Australia are uncertain which number in an English address refers to the flat and which to the building. Finally, the address is not divided line by line as is the case in English. Stamps are placed either on the front or on the back of the envelope.

For official purposes, the envelope may well be of greater importance than the letter it contains. For example, when prospective students are seeking official permission to come to Australia to study, they need to provide evidence that they have been accepted by an Australian institution. In proving this, the envelope in which the letter of acceptance is enclosed is as important as the letter itself. This is because the envelope has the name and address of the recipient on it and therefore testifies that the person receiving the letter is in fact the person referred to in the correspondence. Chinese are therefore likely to attribute equal importance to envelopes received in Australia.

It should also be remembered that in China the signature on a letter is less important than the seal or stamp of the work unit (the company or organisation the person who receives the letter works for). The seal guarantees the contents of the letter in a way that an individual signature is unable to do.

Age and date of birth

When writing dates, the order is the reverse of that used in Australia; the year precedes the month which precedes the day. So a person born on 4 January 1951 would write this date as 1951.1.4.

Traditionally, when calculating ages, Chinese start from one. That is, a baby is reckoned to be one as soon as it is born. Another year is added each Spring Festival (Chinese New Year), so a child born on the day before Chinese New Year is two years old, two days after birth. Officially, the western system is used, but this may cause confusion to some people. One northern teacher who took up a university position in the south reported that even young and educated city dwellers in the south may be unaware of the difference between the two systems and consequently encounter difficulties in filling in forms such as visa applications.

Occupation

For official purposes, a person's work unit (the company or organisation they work for) is usually more important than their actual occupation. Official forms usually require details of both.

When asked about actual occupation, a person is likely to be rather more vague than would be the case in English. Typical answers would be 'I'm a worker/technician/clerk', and so on. More information on occupations can be found in Chapter 5, page 63.

Ethnicity

The vast majority of Chinese nationals are ethnic Han. There are also 55 recognised national minorities, together comprising somewhat less than 5 per cent of the population.

Classroom Tasks

■ TASK 1 ■

Open a telephone book to any page. How many family names are listed on that page? Make a list of them. Compare your list with that of other students. How many other English family names do you already know? Write them down.

■ TASK 2 ■

Use your dictionaries to look up the meaning of your name in English. Explain your name to your partner or your teacher.

■ TASK 3 ■

Write each of the names below in the correct column; that is, boys' names, girls' names and family names. The first one is done for you.

Paul   Sam   Mark

Smith   Jennifer   Susan

Baker   Stephen   Hickson

Christine Carter   Peter

Keith   Barbara   Wright

Boys' names	Girls' names	Family names
Paul		

How many other English names can you add to the lists?

■ TASK 4 ■

Form a group with three other students.

a. What do your names mean in English?

b. Why did your parents choose your name?

Choose a representative from the group to tell one student's story to the class.

Ask your teacher how Australian children usually get their names.

a. What do parents think about when they choose a name?

b. How did your teacher get his or her name?

■ **TASK 5** ■

In 1987, the Federal Government of Australia proposed introducing a national identity card for all Australians. This proposal caused immediate protest from all sections of the community and finally the Federal Government decided to drop the idea.

From what you know of Australian culture, why do you think Australians opposed the identity card proposal?

In groups of three or four list as many reasons for Australians to oppose the proposal as you can think of.

Terms of address

Age and status differences tend to be more clearly marked in Chinese terms of address than they are in English.

The use of given names is confined to family and very close friends. Outside the family, extensive use is made of occupational titles together with the family name when addressing people:

Shi	–	'Teacher'
Wang	–	'Engineer'
Li	–	'Technician'
Gao	–	'Director'

This form of address is primarily used in formal situations, when the speakers are not well acquainted, or when a subordinate is speaking to a superior. In less formal situations at work, when the speakers are well acquainted or when a superior is addressing a subordinate, people are addressed by attaching affectionate diminutives to the family name. Those who are in their late 30s or older are usually addressed as *lao*, 'old', while younger people are addressed as *xiao*, 'young', 'small'. Using a name alone without any term of address sounds extremely impolite and, not surprisingly, many students are therefore reluctant to call their teachers by their given names when they come to Australia.

Other common terms of address are *tongzhi*, 'comrade' and *shifu*, 'master'. The former is, of course, the politically correct form of address and can be used regardless of age or status differences. It has, however, largely gone out of fashion, especially among urban dwellers. 'Master' can be used when addressing shop assistants or in factories when addressing people in authority on the factory floor – supervisors, for example. The term can also be used with any tradesperson.

There are also terms to equate to the English 'Mr', 'Mrs' and 'Miss'. These were frowned on during the years of revolution and even more so during the Cultural Revolution but have since made a comeback.

Within the family, people are often addressed using a title that signifies the relationship between the speakers, 'younger sister' for example, or 'father's younger brother'.

Separate terms exist for paternal and maternal relatives, with paternal relatives being considered closer. Nicknames are often used for young children. Parents are never addressed by their names, always by their relationship titles, 'mother' or 'father'.

Friends usually call each other by family name with one of the diminutives mentioned above, *xiao* or *lao*. Nicknames are also extensively used, these nicknames often differing from the ones used within the family. Given names are only used by very close friends. Their use by others sounds uncomfortably intimate. Many Chinese people adopt western given names when interacting with English speakers in order to avoid the discomfort that is associated with the use of their Chinese given name by non-intimates. When talking to acquaintances rather than friends, the full name is used.

Finally, the option of using no name at all when talking to someone is far less available in Chinese than it is in English. When addressing a stranger it is necessary to use a title, whereas in English neither name nor title would be used. For example, when approaching someone on the street the most commonly used phrase is *qing wen xiansheng*, which roughly translates as 'Excuse me, sir'. Students may therefore use titles inappropriately when speaking English. Another commonly encountered example is the tendency of many students to use the title 'Teacher' to attract attention or to directly address a teacher.

Pronouns

Chinese has two words for the second person singular: *ni* and *nin*. *Nin* is a polite form used with people of much higher status or greater age than the speaker. This term can also be used to address parents, especially in the north. *Ni*, the less respectful term, is used with friends, colleagues, people of a similar age, younger people and subordinates.

As well, there are two words for the first person plural, one of which is used when addressing a group of close friends in an informal situation.

Family relationships

While the traditional picture of the extended Chinese family of several generations all living under one roof was always an ideal realised only by a few wealthy families, it is true that 'family' tends to be rather more broadly defined than is often the case in Australia. The average city-dwelling Chinese family today consists of mother, father, one child and often one or two grandparents. Since the mid-1970s a strict birth-control policy has limited each couple to one child, and the housing crisis means that many married couples must look after either maternal or paternal grandparents. Grandparents are usually expected to look after the child while mother and father are at work. In the past, and especially during the Cultural Revolution, it was not uncommon for grandparents to take complete charge of the child or children as parents were sent to the countryside to take part in manual labour. This type of separation is rare in cities today, but now happens more frequently in the countryside, as men are forced to leave their homes in the impoverished provinces of the interior to seek work in the rapidly developing coastal cities. The same is true of women, though to a lesser degree for married women with children.

Classroom Tasks

■ TASK 1 ■

Read the article and complete the exercises below:

What do I call you?

Most Australians have three names, the first two of which are chosen by the parents when a child is born. These first and second names are called the 'first names', 'given names' or 'Christian names'. The last name is the family name; it comes from the father and is most frequently given to all his children. The family name can also be called the 'surname' or the 'last name'. Here is an example.

John Paul   Smith

Given names   Family name
First names   Surname
Christian names   Last name

Some people have only one given name and some have several, but most people usually have two.

In Australia, people usually call each other by their first name. That is, friends call each other by their first name and employers call their employees by their first name. Many employees also call their employers by their first name. When they meet someone for the first time it is also common for Australians to immediately use the first name. Differences in age are usually not important in deciding what to call someone. Most Australians would still use first names even when the person they are talking to is much older.

There are, however, some times when first names are not used. For example, it is rare for children to call their parents by first name and they would usually call other adults 'aunt' or 'uncle' together with the first name. In some formal situations, such as interviews for jobs or important business meetings, it is also usual not to use first names. Instead a title is used together with the family name.

Four titles are most commonly used. They are:

Mr   –   for a man
Ms   –   for a woman
Mrs   –   for a married woman
Miss –   for an unmarried woman

'Ms' is a new title that has been introduced in the last 20 years. It is very useful as it can be used for both single and married women.

Using these titles, Peter Michael Long is Mr Long and Susan Margaret Carter is Ms (or Mrs or Miss) Carter. It is not common practice to use a title with a first name, nor can we address someone as 'Mr' or 'Ms' without any name at all.

Some titles refer to people's jobs. The most common are:

Doctor   –   for a medical doctor or for a person who has the degree of Doctor of Philosophy (PhD)

Professor   –   for the head of a university department.

Australians do no not use other occupations as titles. They do not say 'Teacher Smith' or 'Engineer Brown'. Shop assistants and other service personnel may address women as 'Madam' and men as 'Sir'.

If you are not sure what to call someone, ask them! They will usually be happy to tell you. Also listen to people around you. You can learn a lot from noticing how people address each other. Most importantly, don't be afraid of making mistakes!

a. According to the article, how should you address the following people:

Michael Robert Johnson	–	your friend
Jane Carol Archer	–	a doctor
Thomas Mawson	–	your superior at work
Sandra Anne Roberts	–	a woman 20 years older than you
David Craig Parker	–	an employer interviewing you for a job
Louise Arnott	–	your teacher
Bruce Donald Williams	–	a professor at the University of Melbourne
Jennifer Short	–	a woman you have just met at a party.

b. Are there any differences between how Australians address each other and how Chinese address each other? Explain the differences to your teacher. Tell your teacher how you would address the people referred to in **Question a** if you were speaking Chinese.

■ TASK 2 ■

During the next week, listen to people around you, to people at work or at school or university, on the bus or train, in shops, on the street. How do they address each other?

Make a larger copy of the following form and fill it in according to how people address each other. Try and get as many examples as possible. At the end of the week, bring back your completed form and compare your findings with those of other students.

An example has been done for you.

Place	Sex	Age	Relationship	Term used
On the bus	F F	young mother small child	mother daughter	First name (Kim) Mum

Aunts, uncles and cousins also play an important role in family life, and together with parents and grandparents form a network that ideally functions to protect and aid family members throughout life.

If the primary relationship within Australian families tends to be that of husband and wife, with children being conceived of as independent individuals from an early age, this is not so in Chinese families. Here, primary stress tends to be on the parent–child relationship. Individuals are first and foremost mothers and fathers rather than husbands and wives. Parents are treated with great respect and are often addressed using the honorific form of the second person singular rather than by the common term. Parents, in particular the father, make all important decisions on their child's behalf, usually until the child gets married. It is, for example, the father who usually decides what subjects his child should study and to what university or other educational institution they should apply. Marriages usually need to be sanctioned by the parents, though parents seldom today (in the cities) arrange a match for their children. There is little opportunity for unmarried children to leave home and live independently. However, many young people are required to live in dormitories provided by their educational institution or work unit. They would normally return to the family home on Saturday night. This does not prevent the common Australian practice of children voluntarily moving out of the family home before marriage being seen by many as evidence that Australians don't really care about their families.

Children are not generally expected to work while they are studying either at school or at university. This expectation often extends to household chores; parents expect students to devote their entire energy to their studies and so children are usually excused from all or most household duties. As this attitude often extends right up to marriage, many young people find the start of married life a shock. For the first time they have to cook and clean for themselves. Young people coming alone to Australia, especially to study, face a similar situation.

There is also no counterpart to the Australian high school student who works during the summer holidays. However, some university students are now supporting themselves by working part-time, for example, offering private tuition in various subjects.

Such efforts were initially greeted with shock and accusations of greed, but are now more widely accepted.

Parents are in general, however, expected to provide extensive financial support for their children. Tertiary study is often financed by the parents, though some help in the form of scholarships is available. Many parents continue to provide support even after the child has entered the workforce, allowing the child to save money for their wedding. Parents are also likely to contribute largely to the cost of buying a flat for the newly weds, and to the cost of furnishing it. There is no expectation that such money would be repaid, that it was merely a loan. In fact, the idea of paying back money to parents sounds shocking and often implies a lack of love and family feeling.

The state of childhood and of dependence tends to last much longer in the Chinese family than it does in the Australian family. In fact, a child tends to remain 'a child' in the Chinese family right up to marriage and it is precisely this state of dependence that is regarded by many Chinese as the true expression of real family feeling. Parents are seen as ready to sacrifice everything to protect their children and ensure their comfort and wellbeing. Consequently, the Australian emphasis on the nurturing of independence from an early age can appear as an abdication of the most basic of parental responsibilities. Having said this, it is also important to remember that attitudes are changing rapidly, particularly in the urban, educated middle class, some members of which have been influenced by western concepts of individualism.

If the parents have a strong obligation to support their children well into adult life, children have equally strong obligations towards their parents' welfare, particularly in later life. As has already been mentioned, children are under a strong obligation to respect and obey their parents, this being a partial return for the love, care and attention bestowed by parents. However, once parents age, the children also have an absolute obligation to look after them, providing them not only with food and shelter but also with love. This means that parents expect to live with their children rather than alone in old age. Old people's homes exist only for those unfortunates who have no children. The proliferation of retirement villages and old people's homes in Australia tends to be seen as yet another proof that Australian family relationships are weak and lack feeling.

Another obligation that children owe to their parents is the obligation to marry and have children. This ensures that the family line will continue and that the parents will have someone to look after them in their old age. However, here again middle class attitudes show signs of changing in the direction of western middle class norms. In particular, an increasing number of educated women are delaying having a family and some are deciding not to have a family at all.

When in need of help or assistance of any kind, it is usual to turn first and foremost to the family, especially to the extended family. It is expected that family members such as uncles, aunts, cousins and remoter kin, as well as brothers and sisters, will use whatever influence they have, for example, to secure a good job, a better flat or access to a scarce commodity, for other family members. (This is discussed in greater detail in Chapter 7, page 107.) Such obligations are of course mutual. Money lent to other family members would usually not have to be repaid. However, the obligation incurred by borrowing money would remain.

Terms for family relationships

Chinese distinguishes between paternal and maternal relatives, as has already been noted. There are therefore different terms, for example, for maternal and paternal grandmothers.

A further distinction is made between younger and older. Where English has the two terms 'brother' and 'sister', Chinese has 'older brother', 'younger brother', 'older sister' and 'younger sister'.

Terms for uncles and aunts reflect these two distinctions. There are separate terms for 'father's elder brother', 'father's younger brother', 'mother's elder brother' and so on. In talking about relatives, then, it is possible to be a great deal more specific about the exact nature of the relationship than is the case in English. The word 'cousin', for example, covers what are several quite distinct relationships in Chinese.

> Parents in western countries don't love their children like Chinese do, and children abandon their parents as soon as possible.
>
> Widespread Chinese belief
>
> How do you account for this strongly entrenched attitude?

Classroom Tasks

■ TASK 1 ■

Read the following 'Letter to the Editor' and answer the questions below.

Dear Sir,

What is going on? Australians used to value independence and individualism. Now it seems that we are turning into a nation of parasites. A report by the Australian Institute of Family Studies shows that children are not leaving home until well into their 20s. There are even some 30-year-olds who are still living with their parents.

What is the matter with these people? How could they be content to bludge off their parents' hard work? We are in danger of producing a generation without self-reliance, without self-respect. If they can't look after themselves, how will they cope with the inevitable problems of life?

Let's get back to the old ways, when young people valued their independence.

Yours sincerely,
Mary Jackson, Newtown.

a. What change does the writer claim is taking place in Australian family life?

b. Does the writer support the change? Why or why not?

c. What does the letter tell you about attitudes to family life in Australia?

d. How do these attitudes compare with Chinese attitudes to family life?

■ TASK 2 ■

Draw your family tree. Include all your family.

Next to each person, write their relationship to you in English and in Chinese.

Are there any terms that do not translate directly into English?

■ TASK 3 ■

Below you will find a survey on Australian family life. Read through the survey and answer questions according to your own idea of Australian families.

Then ask three Australians to complete the survey. You can ask teachers, friends, workmates, neighbours or anyone else you know to help you.

Bring your completed survey sheets back to class and compare your results with those of other students.

Do the results agree with your predictions?

What conclusions can you draw about Australian family life?

Survey: Australian family attitudes

1. Age: Under 20 ☐   30–39 ☐   50–59 ☐
            20–29 ☐   40–49 ☐   over 60 ☐

2. Sex: Male ☐   Female ☐

3. In your family, do the children live with the parents? _____

    If yes, how old are the children? _____

    If no, approximately how old were the children when they left home? _____

4. If the children no longer live at home, how often do they visit their parents?

    Weekly ☐   Fortnightly ☐   Monthly ☐   Other _____

5. What types of activity does the family do together? _____

6. How often does the family do things together? _____

7. If the parents give adult children money, should that money be paid back?

    Why or why not? _____

8. If the family is going on holiday, who decides where they will go?

    Father   ☐

    Father and mother together ☐

    Father, mother and children ☐

9. In deciding what subjects a child should study in the last two years of school, who should make the final decision?

    Father   ☐

    Mother   ☐

    Father and mother   ☐

    Father, mother and child   ☐

    Child alone   ☐

10. What is the most important thing that parents should teach their children?

Friendship and leisure

We have looked at how officialdom sees people and how people relate within their families. We now turn to how people relate to their friends, what they expect from them, what kind of activities they do together and how they treat each other.

> Australians don't really form strong friendships. They are too concerned with themselves and don't care much about others.
>
> Chinese student, Sydney
>
> Why do you think many Chinese would form this impression of Australian friendship?

Friendship

The question 'What are the rights and obligations of friendship?' is a question that is usually not asked. Like many other aspects of Australian social life, friendship is taken for granted. How to relate to and interact with friends is not something Australians consciously learn, it is something they do without asking how or why. It's natural, they feel, and universal: everyone has friends and so naturally everyone behaves the same way towards them. While the former is obviously true for both Australian and Chinese, it is from subtle differences in assumptions about the nature of friendship that major misconceptions and miscommunications arise.

Given that Chinese culture emphasises the interdependence of family members and that little or no assistance is available from official sources in the event of difficulties, it is not surprising that for many Chinese the major obligation of friendship is support. True friends are expected to be prepared to offer not only mental or moral support but also a wide range of help and assistance. Such assistance includes the use of influence to help secure access to scarce resources and to find ways around regulations, help in arranging contacts with others who might be similarly useful, and, ultimately, financial support where and when needed. The extent to which a person offers assistance of course depends on the degree of friendship, and the ideal of total support (or, as many informants put it, total willingness to sacrifice) is perhaps realised in a comparatively rare number of cases. However, this is the standard by which commitment and friendship tend to be judged.

Friendship also involves the giving of moral or mental support and advice in times of difficulty. In Australia, such support would usually be aimed at helping the recipient articulate his or her own desires; in China the emphasis tends to fall more on the giving of advice. There is little or no attempt to discover the wishes, hidden or otherwise, of the person involved. In fact, questions such as 'What do you think?', 'What do you want to do?', frequently employed when Australians are discussing such problems, may sound to a Chinese like an abdication of responsibility. After all, it is precisely the difficulty in deciding what to do that usually caused the problem in the first place!

Interactions with friends tend to sound direct, even abrupt, to Australian ears. If interactions with superiors and strangers tend to be more formal than would be the case in Australia, interactions with friends are much more informal. Chinese often comment on the frequency with which Australians apologise to their friends for minor inconveniences – telephoning late at night or asking someone to help in some way, for example. They also notice that Australians tend to use polite forms such as 'could you ...' and 'would you mind ...' even with close friends. In Chinese, more direct forms are usually used between friends. This sometimes results in Chinese appearing to be too direct or demanding when addressing Australians they know well. At the same time, they may interpret Australians as distant and cold in their friendships.

Classroom Tasks

■ TASK 1 ■

Read the case study below. What do you think the problem is?

Yang Ruifang worked as a secretary in an Australian company. She became friendly with one of the Australian secretaries, a woman called Cathy Lane. The two usually ate lunch together and Yang Ruifang often asked Cathy for advice on problems she faced adjusting to Australian society. Cathy gave her a lot of advice, helped her move house and went with her to the Immigration Bureau several times to help sort out some problems. Yang Ruifang visited Cathy several times at home but did not invite Cathy to her flat because she shared it with four other people. If they did not see each other at the weekend, they usually talked on the phone. As Yang Ruifang was also preparing to take an English test, she was able to get a lot of help with English in this way.

However, something seemed to be going wrong. Cathy seemed to be getting impatient, even a little cold. She started going out by herself at lunchtime instead of eating with Yang Ruifang and seemed reluctant to answer questions. Yang Ruifang was puzzled. She couldn't imagine what the problem was.

a. What do you think the problem was?

b. What do Australians expect from their friends?

c. What advice would you give Yang Ruifang and Cathy Lane in order to restore their friendship?

■ TASK 2 ■

Below are two comments about friendship. The first is an opinion held by many Australians who have lived in China. The second is often said by Chinese in Australia.

Chinese people don't have real friends. They just use people. All they are interested in is what someone can do for them.

Australians don't really form strong friendships. They are too concerned with themselves and don't care much about others.

Do you agree with these comments?

Why do you think these comments are often made?

■ TASK 3 ■

Below are several statements about friends and friendship. Rank them in order from most important to least important.

a. A friend listens to your problems.

b. A friend gives you good advice.

c. A friend lends money if you need it.

d. A friend uses his influence to help you.

e. A friend shares his belongings.

f. A friend shares your likes and dislikes.

g. A friend often helps you do things.

h. A friend tells you when you are wrong.

i. A friend puts business second.

j. A friend lies to protect you.

Now ask an Australian to do the same.

a. Are there any major differences between your answers and the Australian's answers?

b. What differences can you see between Australian and Chinese ideas of friendship?

■ TASK 4 ■

Fill in the following table yourself, then ask Australians for their replies.

A = agree   **D** = disagree   **?** = not sure

Question	Chinese			Australian		
	A	**D**	**?**	**A**	**D**	**?**
1. If I lent $5 to a friend, I would expect them to return it quickly.						
2. If I went to lunch with a group of friends, I would expect that we would split the bill.						
3. If I had a friend working in a government department, I would expect special treatment from that department.						
4. If friends had their own business, I would expect to pay a lower price for their goods.						
5. If I were working in a company that had a vacancy, I would recommend a friend for the job.						
6. If I had a problem, I would want to discuss it with my friend.						
7. If I had a problem, I would listen to my friend's advice.						
The most important duty of a friend is:						

Compare your answers with those of the rest of the class.

a. Are there any major differences between the two sets of answers?

b. What conclusions do you draw about Australian and Chinese friendships?

Leisure activities

While middle class urban dwellers in both Australia and China have a wide range of entertainment options open to them, there are some differences in how, broadly speaking, each group chooses to spend its leisure time. In so far as it is possible to generalise about two such large and diverse groups, it might be said that Australians centre more on their social life about the home than would be the case in China. As an example, let us take three common Australian leisure activities. Dinner parties, barbecues and parties are likely to figure fairly prominently on most Australian social calendars. In China, the fact that most people live in small apartments without individual gardens means that such activities are more difficult to organise than in Australia, and so are very much less common. They may, however, be organised in settings outside the home. For example, university students often organise parties which may be for students of a particular class or year or may be open to all students. These parties are usually held in classrooms or university halls and have the support of the university authorities.

Barbecues and picnics are becoming more popular, and usually take place at scenic spots. However, the choice of food, and particularly the choice of meat to be barbecued, may be rather different. Steak and sausages are unlikely to be featured on the menu! In fact, one young Chinese woman graphically described her first Australian barbecue in the following terms:

I really remember my first barbecue. They put this huge piece of meat on a fire and when it was all black on the outside they gave it to me and I had to eat it and it was … lots of blood … red. Just this big … piece … meat!

Dinner parties are not at all common in China, so Chinese invited to Australian dinner parties may be unaware of some of the conventions surrounding them. This refers especially to the choice of an appropriate gift and to the time at which it is appropriate to arrive and leave. Some may be unused to using western cutlery, especially if the meal is elaborate and a range of knives and forks is used.

One form of the dinner party may be especially unfamiliar, and that is the potluck dinner. Many Chinese would expect the host of a dinner party to provide all the food. In addition, once they become used to potlucks, they may overgeneralise and take a cooked dish to a dinner party, an occurrence which has caused consternation to more than one host.

One way of socialising that is shared between the two cultures is going out to a restaurant for a meal, but even here there are differences. Most middle class Australians are used to eating a wide range of cuisines, while the majority of Chinese tend to be happier with one of the many styles that constitute Chinese cuisine. This does not mean that Chinese do not eat other cuisines, rather that their tastes are somewhat less eclectic than those of their Australian counterparts.

Splitting the bill is another aspect of the Australian restaurant experience that many Chinese are likely to find problematic. When dining with friends, one person is likely to pay, knowing that on another occasion someone else will do so. In the event that one person is generally perceived as being somewhat better off than all the others in the group, he or she may end up paying more often. This is especially so among young people. The Australian custom of each person contributing a proportion of the bill, or, worse, calculating exactly how much each person owes is likely to appear mean and even miserly to many Chinese.

Much of Chinese social life is self-organised and does not depend on organised venues. Public spaces such as parks are intensively used. Couples meet in them, married couples take their toddlers to play in them, friends talk, old people practice opera and tai chi. Many parks have facilities for boating, and provide areas where groups can practice martial arts, music, ballroom dancing and other activities that would be carried out inside in Australia. In summer, social life in older areas spills into the street to avoid the heat indoors, but there is a strong cultural preference for pale skin, so most women take care to protect their skin from the sun by wearing hats and often carrying umbrellas. In Australia, this attitude helps to explain the many Chinese girls who venture on to the beach wearing what Australians regard as street wear; skirts, blouses and shoes. It is also true that many young girls are reluctant to expose themselves to public view in swimming costumes.

Shopping, or at least window shopping, is an extremely popular leisure activity and one that has received an enormous boost in recent years from the huge number of shopping malls and department stores that have sprung up in all major cities. Many people have hobbies – stamp collecting and playing musical instruments being among the most popular. With regard to the latter, Chinese culture tends to stress participation to a much greater extent than does Australian culture. This means that people are expected to perform in public, at class parties for example. When called upon to perform, usually to sing, most people would initially decline, but would then gracefully give in to renewed requests. It also means that an expression of interest in an art form may be taken to mean that the person in question can actually perform.

Sport is extremely popular; though, as in Australia, spectator sport predominates. Soccer has a particularly strong following; Manchester United is reputed to have more supporters in China than in the whole of Europe. Basketball is also very popular, particularly as Chinese players are beginning to appear in American basketball teams.

The most popular participant sports tend to be individual sports such as jogging, tai chi (for older people) and martial arts. A lack of facilities and land tends to restrict team sports to those requiring little space and few facilities – table tennis and volleyball fall into this category. In general, participation in sport is informal and unorganised. The network of community-based sporting clubs that exists in Australia has no counterpart in China.

The last few years have seen an explosion in part-time study, with huge numbers of people, especially young people, enrolling in classes in foreign languages and computing. Recently courses in business, accounting and foreign trade have also become popular.

Evening entertainment includes karaoke bars and pubs. Discos and other dance venues are also popular, though the music they play tends to be softer and more romantic than western dance music. The government keeps a wary eye on manifestations of pop culture and shuts down bands and venues that are deemed to have gone too far.

One further difference that needs to be mentioned relates to alcohol. Alcohol is socially acceptable in China as it is in Australia, but patterns of usage differ quite considerably. In recent years young middle class women have started to drink, and western-style wines enjoy some degree of popularity. Cocktails are also popular among those young people who frequent bars and discos. However, perhaps the most popular and widely consumed form of alcohol, especially among men, is beer.

Chinese spirits tend to be much stronger than Australian ones and are drunk neat, accompanied by small snacks. When wine or spirits are served at important meals or banquets, they are usually drunk only when toasts are proposed, rather than being sipped throughout the meal as would be the case in Australia. Beer and soft drinks are provided for sipping.

Classroom Tasks

■ TASK 1 ■

Quick Quiz – Social customs

How much do you know about social life in Australia? Try this quick quiz.

1. You go out to a restaurant with a group of friends. Who pays?

    a. You split the bill ☐

    b. One person pays ☐

2. You are invited to a dinner party for eight o'clock. What time do you arrive?

    a. Quarter to eight ☐

    b. Quarter past eight ☐

    c. Any time ☐

    d. Eight o'clock ☐

3. What type of gift would you take to a dinner party?
    (You can tick more than one box.)

    a. Some Chinese food that you cooked yourself ☐

    b. A bottle of wine ☐

    c. A box of chocolates ☐

    d. An expensive scarf ☐

4. The party starts at eight o'clock. You've missed the train and won't arrive until nine. Do you:

    a. Not worry. It's a party, not a dinner party, and people can arrive whenever they like. ☐

    b. Telephone, apologise and tell your host you'll be late. ☐

    c. Go home. You don't want to arrive late and you're too embarrassed to telephone. ☐

5. You're invited to a picnic in a national park, but at the last minute some urgent business comes up. Do you:

    a. Go anyway. You promised to go so you must go. ☐

    b. Telephone your host and apologise, explaining that some urgent business has arisen. ☐

    c. Just don't go. Lots of other people are going so it doesn't matter if you don't go. ☐

6. It's ten-thirty at night but you have an important message for your Australian friend. Do you:

   a. Telephone and give them the message. ☐

   b. Telephone, apologise for disturbing them and give them the message. ☐

   c. Wait until tomorrow. Ten-thirty is too late to telephone. ☐

7. You're at a party and you're offered something to drink. You say:

   a. No thanks, I'm not very thirsty. ☐

   b. Thanks. I'll have a Coke. ☐

   c. Sorry. I don't drink alcohol. ☐

   d. Could I have a beer? ☐

8. You're at a dinner party and you don't like some of the food. Do you:

   a. Eat a little anyway, to be polite. ☐

   b. Explain that you're not used to Australian food and so can't eat it. ☐

   c. Say that you are not hungry because you ate before you came. ☐

9. A friend introduces you to a local couple and you enjoy talking to them. They give you their address and ask you to drop in some time. Do you:

   a. Visit their house a couple of days later. ☐

   b. Wait a few days and give them a ring. ☐

   c. Never contact them again. ☐

10. You and your wife have a local friend who invites you to a party on Saturday evening. Who goes?

   a. You go alone. ☐

   b. You and your wife go together. ☐

   c. You, your wife and your five-year-old son go. ☐

■ TASK 2 ■

Ask a group of Australians the following questions about eating habits. Then ask the same questions of an equal number of Chinese from different parts of China.

Do Chinese from different parts of the country have similar eating habits?

How do these eating habits compare with those of Australians?

Summarise your findings on a poster and share them with your class.

a. What are the main meals of the day?

b. At approximately what times are these meals eaten?

c. What is the most important meal of the day?

d. What type of food is eaten at each meal?

e. Does the family eat each meal together?

f. Is it normal to talk at meals?

g. How often do people eat in restaurants?

h. Is eating in restaurants a popular leisure activity?

■ TASK 3 ■

An Australian couple are going to live in China for two years. As they are friends of yours, they have asked you to write them some notes about social life in China. They particularly want to know what people do in their spare time, for example on Sunday or in the evenings.

In groups, write a brief report for them, being sure to answer the following questions:

a. Do people usually go out in groups, as couples or as individuals? Do families do things together?

b. What type of activities are popular on Saturday evenings?

c. Do people like eating in restaurants or having dinner parties?

d. Is playing sport popular? If so, what sports, where and when?

e. If people stay at home, what do they do?

f. What differences do you notice with Australian leisure activities?

When you have finished your report, compare it to the reports of other groups.

Give your report to an Australian friend. What differences does that friend see between leisure activities in Australia and in China?

■ TASK 4 ■

Some people say that Australia is a boring place because there's nothing to do. Is this true?

a. Ask five different Australians what they do on Saturdays and Sundays.

b. Australian newspapers often publish special entertainment guides once a week. Look at one of these guides from the major newspaper in your city.

- How many different classifications can you find? (For example, films, classes, etc.)

- Choose three different activities that you would like to do. What do you have to do to take part in them?

- Many radio stations have Community Information Hotlines. These hotlines give information on entertainment. Look up the number of one of the radio stations in your area, ring their Hotline and note down three activities that are happening in your city this weekend.

- Look up the Clubs section of the phone book. How many different sections are there?

On the basis of the information you collect in these three areas, write a brief report for a Chinese newspaper on social life and leisure activities in Australia.

Meeting people

When we meet someone informally for the first time we attempt to find out certain things about them. The conversation tends to focus on a number of standard 'safe' topics, topics that are unlikely to be perceived by either party as threatening. These topics help us to classify the person we are talking to, allowing us to establish, for example, their social position, perhaps something of their character, or maybe whether we would like to continue the acquaintance. What it is that we are trying to find out, and the topics that allow us to do so in a non-threatening manner, vary from culture to culture, and these variations frequently result in serious miscommunication. Consider, for example, hostility many Australians feel when asked some of the questions that are a standard part of introductory conversation in many cultures:

How old are you?
Are you married?
How many children have you got?

Answers to these questions constitute essential information in many cultures, information without which it is difficult to establish the social position and role of the unknown party. This is important because without this information, people do not know how to address a stranger without appearing rude. This is discussed in greater detail in the section on hierarchy in Chapter 7, page 109. In Australia, this type of information is classified as personal rather than essential, age and family situation not being seen as central to the establishment of a relationship between two strangers.

In China, however, family relationships and roles continue to be 'essential information', that is, information that everyone seeks to give and get on first meeting. This means that questions about age, marital status and number of children are quite common, especially when differences in age and status are involved. For example, an older person would frequently ask such questions of a younger person, as would a younger person of an older person. A young man would not, however, ask a young woman whether she were married. Such a question has a similar meaning in both cultures. In such a case, the information would be found out indirectly.

Another question closely connected to family background is, 'Where do you come from?' There are alternative answers to this question, which may refer to the town or city in which the speaker currently resides, but which may equally refer to the town or village from which the speaker's family comes. In this case, the speaker may in fact never have visited the place in question, but as it is the ancestral home, it is also the place from which they come.

On first meeting, people are also likely to ask about occupation, but the emphasis tends to be on the work unit rather than on the actual occupation. Questions about salary are also permitted. Other common job-related questions concern mutual acquaintances. People often attempt to find relatives, classmates or other acquaintances working in the same work unit. It would be unusual to ask whether a job was enjoyable or not. In fact, this question, when asked in English, tends to provoke a certain amount of confusion as people are not sure what type of answer is expected.

Personal interests also play a far smaller role in introductory conversations than they do in Australia.

Casual conversation

Although it may seem to Australians that everyday casual conversation is spontaneous and unplanned and that the choice of topic is determined by individual preference, in fact many cultures appear to use a relatively narrow range of topics as 'preferred topics' in casual conversation. Preferred topics are those that people are most likely to select when talking informally to friends and acquaintances. Preferred topics naturally vary from culture to culture, and people's reactions to others' selections tend to reflect the values of their own culture. Many Chinese, for example, consider Australians' preference for talking about their own interests and activities to be unduly self-absorbed and even selfish.

As we have just remarked, for Australians personal activities and interests form the basis of much of their everyday conversation, as the frequency of questions such as 'What did you do at the weekend?' attests. This focus on personal interests in general and weekend activities in particular is largely absent in Chinese daily conversation. Many Chinese learners of English are therefore uncertain how to reply to questions about weekend activities, as they are not sure what is expected of them.

Chinese casual conversation often focuses on the activities of others rather than the activities of those taking part in the conversation. Another common topic, especially among women, is shopping and the price of goods. Sport is popular as a topic with men. The conversation of Chinese living in Australia, especially those who have been here for a comparatively short time, tends to be dominated by topics such as the inefficiency of public transport and the strange customs of Australians. Food is a perennial topic for everyone.

In general, the point to remember is that in learning English, Chinese students may well be unsure about what to talk about as well as how to talk about it. Teachers need to consider how best to prepare students for the topics they are most likely to encounter in everyday conversation. Preparation includes appropriateness of response as well as grammatical accuracy.

When you meet someone for the first time, what do you talk about?

The next time you meet someone new in an informal situation such as at a party, notice what sort of questions you ask each other. Do the same thing when you meet someone new at work.

Are there any differences between what is asked at work and what is asked in less formal circumstances?

Ask others what they ask in similar situations and compare your questions with theirs.

We have noted previously that Chinese students may be unsure about how to answer the common question, 'What did you do at the weekend?'

Design a lesson that focuses on exploring appropriate responses to this question. (Remember to ensure that students understand the reasons for such a lesson.)

Classroom Tasks

■ TASK 1 ■

What do Chinese people talk about when they meet each other for the first time?

Make a larger copy of the worksheet below. The first column is headed 'Informal'. In this column, write down some of the questions that you might ask a person who is introduced to you by a friend in an informal situation.

The second column is headed 'At work'. In this column, write down the questions you might ask someone who has just started working in your workplace.

Informal	At work

a. Are there any questions that you might ask someone of the same sex, but not someone of the opposite sex?

b. Are there any questions that you might ask someone younger than yourself, but not someone older?

Next time you actually do meet someone new, listen to what they ask you and what you ask them. Compare what you wrote with what actually happens.

a. Are there any questions that you didn't mention?

b. What difference does being in a foreign country such as Australia make?

Ask some Australians to fill out the same form and compare their answers with the answers given by Chinese.

■ TASK 2 ■

Sun Zhengrong had been in Australia for only a short time and didn't speak English very well. He didn't like talking to Australians. One day a friend asked him why. He said 'My English is poor. When I talk to Australians, they ask me lots of questions. They ask "Where are you from? What do you do? Where do you live? Do you like Australia?" Lots of questions. I feel like they are policemen. I can't ask them anything. I just have to answer their questions. I can't stand it.'.

What advice would you give Sun Zhengrong to help solve this problem?

Male–female relationships

Great changes are taking place in China in regard to male–female relationships, changes that in many ways parallel the changes that have taken place in Australia over the past 30 years. However, there are still significant differences between China and Australia in attitudes to courtship, marriage and sex.

While the minimum legal age for marriage for women is 20 and for men 22, until mid-2003, very few urban couples were able to obtain the necessary permit from their workplace until the woman was at least 23 and the man 25. However, in mid-2003, a new marriage law was passed which made both marriage and divorce easier and which did away with the necessity for workplaces to agree to the marriage of their employees. How this will affect the age of marriage remains to be seen.

Although professional matchmakers have largely disappeared, it is not uncommon for parents, older relatives and friends to play a role in introducing likely partners to each other. In particular, it is very common for a friend to introduce two people whom he or she feels would be well suited. In such cases, the initial meeting takes place in the company of at least the person making the introduction. Both parties have the right of refusal and only if both parties are willing will the acquaintance be continued.

Among city dwellers, the Internet and introduction agencies have also come to play a significant role in finding a marriage partner in recent years.

Sometimes both young men and young women may ask a friend to accompany them to an introductory or at least an early meeting. They will then discuss the suitability of the intended partner with that friend before deciding whether or not to pursue the acquaintance.

Once two people start going out together it is not easy to terminate the relationship, though this is changing in the big cities. For most people, however, the expectation is that they will eventually get married.

There are of course cases where relationships break up, but the Australian expectation that a person will date several people before developing a serious relationship with one of them is relatively rare. In fact, such an attitude is usually considered immoral by mainstream Chinese society.

If a relationship does develop between two people who have been introduced by a third party, that third party will consider themselves responsible for the relationship and may lose face if it fails.

The prevailing attitude towards women among young people can best be illustrated by a comment made by one of the most prominent of the student leaders during the 1989 protest movement. He came from outside Beijing and when his girlfriend came unexpectedly to join him in Tiananmen Square, he commented that he was of course happy to see her, but didn't actually want her present in the centre of things in Tiananmen because she represented simplicity, peace and pleasure.

Purity, innocence and naivety are therefore the images most often associated with the ideal woman, images captured in countless calendars and thousands of photographs in which young women smile demurely from behind obscuring branches of plum or peach blossom. This is not of course to say that Chinese women are submissive and dependent. However, in terms of the attributes valued in courtship, women who do not at least feign dependence and timidity may find it difficult to attract a partner.

Australian women may appear to many Chinese men to be unduly aggressive and unfeminine. Many would also consider that they are shamefully exploited. This is not so much because of their economic position as because of their perceived sexual exploitation. The open and aggressive use of sex in advertising, the widespread practice of living together before marriage and the publicised incidence of rape all combine to produce a situation in which, it is felt, no woman is safe. Of course sexual crimes also occur in China, but they are vastly under-reported, so the situation in foreign countries is perceived as being especially lawless and dangerous for women.

Marriage is almost universally regarded as natural, necessary and inevitable, and the pressure on people, and especially on women, to get married is inescapable and increasingly strong as a woman nears 30. A woman who is over 30 and still not married is often the target of rumours about her character and/or her mental and physical health. This is also true of men, though to a lesser extent.

The emphasis in the process of getting married differs significantly between Australia and China. In China, the legal registration of the marriage takes place in a government office very similar to a registry office, but this process may take place several weeks or even several months before what is considered to be the actual wedding. The actual wedding is deemed to take place when it is socially legitimised through a party, what an Australian would call a reception, held either at the groom's home or, more usually, in a restaurant. The answer to the question 'Where did you get married?' is therefore usually given as 'In a restaurant' in China.

Weddings are often very lavish, with large amounts of money being spent on them and whole families often going into debt. The bride will normally wear at least three different outfits during the reception, usually including a western-style wedding dress in red, pink or white and a traditional tight-fitting red dress of the type called *cheongsam* in English. The groom usually wears a suit and a red flower. In some rural areas, bridal dresses are replaced by a red silk jacket and a pair of trousers.

Guests present the couple with small red bags or envelopes containing money, red being a symbol of happiness, and special happiness sweets are distributed by the bride and groom.

Among workers and peasants, dowries, provided by the man, are common and often substantial. Many girls are unwilling to marry unless they are assured of being able to move into a newly decorated house or flat. Among educated families, the couple, or rather, the parents of both bride and groom, are far more likely to share the expenses of setting up a house.

Once married, the expectation is that the couple will have children, or rather, under the one-child policy, that they will have a child. Until recently, most cities insisted that couples obtain permission to have their baby, thus regulating the number and distribution of babies born in any one year. Boys are almost universally favoured over girls in all sections of society except amongst intellectuals, because boys are able to carry on the family name. Intellectuals tend to be rather more influenced by ideas relating to the equality of women.

The one-child family is intensively enforced in the cities. Women who do become pregnant for a second time face extreme pressure for an abortion, pressure from their work unit, their neighbours, the local district committees. The pressure is exerted by means of increasingly frequent visits and exhortations to obey the law. At the same time, both husband and wife lose all chance of promotion at work and are often demoted as well. They must also reimburse the state for all allowances and subsidies received for the first child, bear the full cost of bringing up both children and even pay a fine of anywhere between ten and 30 times their annual income. In the circumstances, it is not surprising that in the cities very few couples dare to have a second child.

One result of the one-child policy is that the child, focus of the combined attentions, hopes and dreams of four grandparents and two parents, is often very spoilt. Such children are known as 'little emperors' and people are becoming increasingly anxious about the future effects of such undivided attention. At the same time, in a country where security in old age is largely provided by the children, there is an increasing awareness of the difficulties that are likely to emerge once these 'little emperors' have to shoulder the burden of four aged parents.

Divorce is becoming increasingly common, and recent changes to the marriage law have made it much easier to obtain. The more conservative sections of society still frown upon it, but among middle class Chinese this attitude is changing rapidly.

Sex education has only been introduced in the past few years, and then only on a limited scale. Sexual ignorance is consequently startling in both extent and depth. Sexual relationships are in fact illegal before marriage though this particular law tends, not unnaturally, to be ineffective, except in so far as it deprives single women of access to reliable and safe birth-control measures.

All of the above applies mainly to people living in cities. Peasants in general get married much earlier than city dwellers, regardless of the legal age limits. Indeed, many reports suggest that as many as 85 per cent of country marriages are illegal; that is, not officially registered. This situation arises largely because of the differentiation made between the registration of a marriage and its social validation described above.

The position of women

Apart from the position of women in the family, which has already been examined, we need to touch briefly on the economic position of women. In formal terms, the position of women in Chinese society has vastly improved over the past 40 years. They enjoy the same rights and responsibilities as men, and not only are they encouraged to enter the workforce but their contribution to the family income is crucial. Most urban families depend on a second income to make ends meet.

In spite of formal equality, however, Chinese women often find themselves in a situation similar to that of their Australian sisters. They work, but in order to succeed they need to be twice as good, twice as hard working as their male counterparts. Women are vastly under-represented in the higher reaches of government, the Party, the public service and industry. They are concentrated in professions that are traditionally female and poorly paid, working as teachers, secretaries, in various medical fields (which do not enjoy the prestige granted them in Australia), and in the lower reaches of government and Party service. Many work units are reluctant to employ qualified, even highly qualified, women in responsible posts, as women are considered to be likely to get married and have a child. Married women are expected to focus on their family, or rather on their child, and thus are believed to make poor employees. If a married woman with a child tries to make a career (as opposed to working out of necessity), she may be considered ambitious, a most unfeminine trait!

One problem that has emerged with the growing prosperity of the last decade is that of the second wife. This is particularly prevalent in the south and involves men setting up usually young rural women as mistresses. Both wives and advocates of women's rights object strongly to this practice on the grounds that it involves exploitation of both wife and mistress and drains family resources. The government is also strongly opposed to the trend and has passed legislation mandating jail terms for offenders. This measure has not, however, been very effective.

Add to this the pressure to get married that women face, their powerlessness to control their own fertility and the necessity to take primary responsibility for the smooth running of the home while at the same time holding a job, and the position of Chinese women appears to be a difficult one. It does not, however, differ greatly from the position of Australian women.

Classroom Tasks

■ TASK 1 ■

Fill in the following table yourself and then ask an Australian to answer the questions as well. Compare your answers to the rest of the class.

Do the Australian and the Chinese answers differ? If so, how?

1 = strongly agree   **2** = agree   **3** = undecided   **4** = disagree   **5** = strongly disagree

Male–Female Roles	Chinese					Australian				
	1	**2**	**3**	**4**	**5**	**1**	**2**	**3**	**4**	**5**
1. The man is the head of the family.										
2. The woman should look after the children.										
3. Women should not oppose their husbands.										
4. Men should undertake 50 per cent of the housework.										
5. The husband is primarily responsible for supporting the family.										
6. Married women with young children should work.										
7. The husband should decide on major purchases for the family.										
8. It is unnatural for a woman not to marry.										
9. Husbands and wives should do everything together.										
10. A wife should let her husband make the decisions.										
11. If a husband has a girlfriend, his wife should ignore it.										
12. A wife should fit in with her husband's wishes.										
13. A husband should earn more than his wife.										
14. A woman's career is not as important as a man's.										
15. A wife should be younger than her husband.										

■ TASK 2 ■

By comparison with Australian women, Chinese women are still oppressed, especially in the areas of employment and responsibilities in the home.
Australian resident of Shanghai

Australian women claim to be emancipated, but in fact their social position is lower than that of Chinese women.
Chinese resident of Sydney

a. Do you agree with these statements?

b. Why do you think that the two people involved made them?

c. How would you compare the position of women in Australia and China?

CHAPTER FIVE

LIVING IN SOCIETY

The rapid pace of change in Chinese society over the last ten years means almost every aspect of life has changed beyond recognition. The iron rice bowl, the colloquial term for a system which guaranteed full employment at the price of control over almost every aspect of daily life, has been dismantled. It has been replaced by a way of life not greatly dissimilar to that of people in the English speaking world. This means that in dealing with the issues of employment, housing, shopping, transport and health there are now far fewer differences than was the case a decade ago.

Employment

Over the past 20 years the State Owned Enterprises (SOEs) which once provided cradle-to-grave security for Chinese workers have been reformed, sold off or closed down. They now comprise less than 25 per cent of Chinese companies. In their place, a huge number of new enterprises have arisen, including a significant number of ventures either jointly owned by Chinese and overseas companies or owned outright by international companies. With this change has come the development of a middle class, now estimated to number around 100 million. At the same time, approximately the same number of peasants have left the countryside to look for work in the cities. They form the workforce for the sweat shops that now produce the majority of the world's clothing and footwear. Millions of the workers from the old SOEs have been dismissed or sent home to exist on basic wages that are barely enough to survive on. The picture of employment at the beginning of the third millennium is therefore extremely diverse. It includes young women working up to 16 hours a day for sub-contractors producing well-known brands of sportswear, sleeping in crowded company dormitories and subject to heavy fines for minor infractions of the rules. It also includes young upwardly mobile professionals who live in spacious modern apartments and work for multinational corporations.

Until the beginning of the 1990s, individuals were assigned jobs by the state. This is no longer the case: each person is now responsible for finding his/her own employment. A variety of means exist to help in the search, including job fairs organised by universities and by municipal authorities, Internet job listings, advertisements and *guanxi*. *Guanxi* means personal connections and is treated more fully elsewhere in this volume (see Chapter 7, page 107). In relation to employment, it means the use of personal connections to secure favourable appointments. For example, if a family member is acquainted with someone occupying a position of authority in a company, he or she will approach that person to help obtain a good job for their son or daughter. *Guanxi* is as widely utilised as it is widely resented and cannot be overlooked when considering Chinese attitudes to obtaining jobs.

Finding a position is no longer as easy as it used to be, as more students are graduating from universities and all tend to expect well paid and glamorous jobs with well-known companies rather than the more ordinary middle-management and entry-level professional positions with less well-known companies that tend to be on offer.

Interviews and curriculum vitae

With the shift towards a more competitive market economy, the use of interviews and curriculum vitae (CV) has become much more common in recruitment of personnel. However, this change is occurring at different paces in various parts of the country. In cities like Shanghai the transition is most advanced and hiring practices tend to be closer to those found in the West. In some of the large inland cities such as Chongqing, where the process of reform has been slower, more traditional practices remain influential. The following discussion of attitudes to curriculum vitae and interviews focuses on these more conservative attitudes.

The first question to be discussed relates to the nature and purpose of a curriculum vitae. A request for a curriculum vitae may be interpreted as a request to see copies of qualifications. This is because a Chinese work unit, in evaluating a potential employee, tends to place major emphasis on qualifications. In general, previous experience in a particular job is not accorded the importance it is given by Australian employers.

A related point is that any experience a job seeker does have is likely to be evaluated differently. In many areas of China, stability of employment tends to be the norm and to be highly valued. A job seeker who lists a number of job changes may be regarded as unreliable, unstable and socially undesirable. However, in cities such as Shanghai, this is no longer true as increasing emphasis is being laid on the need for creativity and the ability to deal with the unexpected.

Chinese job seekers may also be reluctant to list the full range of their experience in their curriculum vitae. This refers in particular to experience that they consider not in keeping with their status. University graduates, for example, may prefer not to indicate that they have been working in a factory since arriving in Australia. If they are recent graduates, they may not list any part-time work they undertook to finance their university studies.

Differing attitudes to responsibility and decision making (see Chapter 8, page 131) may result in some Chinese experiencing difficulties in appropriately specifying the duties that they have performed in previous positions. This is especially so if the applicant is unaware of the expectations of Australian employers regarding the attributes and types of experience valued by employers.

The purpose of the interview itself may also be misunderstood. Many people are unaware that a culling process will probably already have taken place and that any people whose qualifications were inadequate would probably not have been invited for an interview. They may therefore believe that the primary purpose of the interview is to establish the authenticity of their qualifications. Alternatively, they may believe that the interview is a formality to be gone through before formally accepting the job. In either case, people tend to be unprepared for the types of questions that are usually asked in an interview.

Firstly, they are often unaware of what the interviewer is looking for. They are inexperienced in analysing the requirements of a job and in matching those requirements to their own experience. Note the primacy here of experience over qualifications.

Secondly, Chinese job seekers are not used to facing questions designed to assess their psychological suitability for the job. Here again they are handicapped by being unaware that the interviewer is probably looking for highly valued traits such as independence, initiative, self-confidence, the ability to work in a team, and the ability to cope in a crisis. Having once realised this, they are still faced with the necessity of displaying the possession of such qualities.

Questions like 'Why do you want this job?' pose particular problems. The Chinese applicant may miss the implied invitation to relate his or her own strengths to the needs and developmental goals of the company. The answer is therefore likely to be couched in terms that relate solely to the individual and to his or her own abilities and interests. Little or no consideration would be given to the interests of the company.

Alternatively, applicants may be reluctant to answer the question on the grounds that it requires a positive evaluation of their own abilities and that this would be unduly boastful. They may feel that such an evaluation can only properly come from others and that the only acceptable way of claiming certain abilities is to give evidence of them in practice. Such an attitude is particularly likely to be found among young women from sheltered and traditional backgrounds.

The opposite problem arises when Chinese applicants learn enough about Australian culture to realise that to talk of one's own abilities is a necessary and accepted part of the interview process. Some people may then become too direct in their approach, resulting in the Australian interviewer perceiving them as boastful or pushy.

Chinese applicants frequently fail to take advantage of the opportunity given at the end of the interview to ask questions. If questions are asked, they usually relate to salary and conditions, but frequently no questions are asked at all. The applicant thus loses a valuable opportunity to display interest in prospects for training, promotion and general upgrading which would demonstrate initiative and readiness to accept a challenge.

A final word needs to be said about the interview panel itself. As it is often composed of several people, all of whom sit behind imposing desks arrayed opposite the applicant, the impact can be quite overwhelming to the inexperienced.

Working conditions

The standard Chinese working week is a five-day 40-hour week. For most middle class professionals, this is a reality, but poorly paid workers, especially those working for sub-contractors to multinational corporations, are expected and indeed forced to work much longer hours. Paid annual leave is still not very common, but public holidays are important. The most significant is Spring Festival or Chinese New Year, as it is known in the West. This occurs in late January or February, depending on the moon and can result in between one and three weeks effective holiday depending on the organisation. Other important public holidays are May Day (1 May) and National Day (1 October).

Wages are, by Australian standards, very low and are usually paid once a month.

In spite of government attempts at reform, workplace safety continues to be very low, with safety guidelines routinely ignored. Workers injured at work usually do not have access to workers compensation or other means of redress.

On the job

Relationships between superior and subordinate in the workplace tend to be rather more formal than is the case in Australia. Managers and directors are addressed by their full names and titles or by family name and title. Subordinates may be similarly addressed. They may also be called by their full name and the use of diminutives with the family name is also acceptable. Supervisors are addressed as *shifu*.

In addressing subordinates, superiors tend to be direct, using orders rather than requests, while subordinates tend to be deferential in return. This does not imply strained or inharmonious relations, but marks status and age differences. In fact, the superior–subordinate relationship involves responsibilities that would not generally form part of a similar relationship in Australia. A superior often acknowledges some sort of responsibility for the welfare of his or her subordinates, a responsibility that might involve offering assistance in times of difficulty, exerting influence on the subordinate's behalf and giving practical and moral advice. An example of the latter would involve counselling in relation to marital difficulties. In return, the subordinate gives loyalty and support.

Advertisement 1

Advertisement 2

EXPERIMENTAL SCIENTIST

$55,748–$65,845

CSIRO
Division of Wool Technology

➤ **General:** The Division of Wool Technology has over 400 staff who run research projects designed to help wool compete in the market place.

➤ **The Position:** The Textile Research Group needs an Experimental Scientist to work on the initiation of a new program of mechanical wool processing. This will involve the use of newly installed equipment and collaboration with the local and overseas wool processing industries.

➤ **The Person:** You are required to be both innovative and practical; good at implementing novel concepts as 'real world' solutions. You should have a physical science degree (or equivalent) and be able to demonstrate a passion for precise measurements.

➤ **Applications:** Applications should relate to the selection criteria and should provide relevant personal details, details of qualifications and experience, and the names of two referees.

Cataloguer – TC 132

THE POSITION

To catalogue new audiovisual and non-fiction resources. Public desk duties, mainly Information and Reference Desks. Other duties as directed by the City Librarian.

QUALIFICATIONS AND EXPERIENCE

Professional library qualifications recognised by ALIA essential. Proven ability to catalogue quickly and accurately is essential. A knowledge of contemporary and classical music would be an advantage. Good communication skills and the ability to work as a member of a team with all levels of staff are essential criteria.

APPLICATIONS

All applications should state qualifications, experience and educational level attained as well as date duties could be commenced. Please provide home and work phone numbers and copies of references if appropriate.

Advertisement 3

OFFICE ASSISTANT

Sun Alliance Life Insurance, a well-established company, is looking for an energetic individual for their busy *Marketing Services Department*. Duties will be varied, including clerical, reception, typing and general office functions.

The position would suit a reliable and organised person who seeks a varied environment. An immediate start is available.

Please direct all inquiries to Sue King on 9777 6666

Advertisement 4

Retail Manager

Australia's newest and brightest athletic footwear and apparel retailer requires the services of an enthusiastic and motivated Manager to join the company. Will be responsible for hiring staff, sales, wages, book work, etc. $50,000 per year. Must be hard-working, enthusiastic and career oriented. Will be fully trained in all aspects of retail management. References and excellent presentation required.

Contact James on 9777 8888

Advertisement 5

Warehouse Coordinator

Pantire Australia P/L is looking for a highly disciplined motivated and enthusiastic individual to join our warehouse team in New Cross. Your main focus would be the guidance of all day to day warehouse operations. The ideal candidate will be a mature minded, experienced, hands-on team player with a demonstrated successful approach. The successful applicant will have substantial warehouse experience, superior people skills, good oral and written skills, computer literacy, be able to prioritise work under pressure and meet deadlines. Send your application with resume to fax 22334455 or email to:
recruit@ pantire.org.au

Advertisement 7

IT Product Manager

Leading manufacturer and distributor of IT products seeks product manager. Bachelor degree and min 5 years experience in marketing of IT products required. Extensive experience in sourcing from Korea and acquaintance with Korean IT companies essential. Salary $50K.

Applications to Director
53–55 Smith Parade, North Sloe, Melbourne 3000

Advertisement 6

Sales Engineer

Electronic Components
Sydney

An experienced Engineer/Technician is required to promote our unique range of semi-conductor products.

Previous sales experience preferred but an enthusiastic technical person with good communication skills would be considered.

If you would like to be part of a dedicated young company, enjoying rapid growth, with an exciting range of leading edge products, call us today.

A salary package commensurate with experience and qualifications will be negotiated.

Contact: Fred Smith
Personnel Manager
Phone: (02) 9222 2222
Fax: (02) 9333 3333

Classroom Tasks

NB: All tasks relate to the advertisements on pages 66 and 67.

■ TASK 1 ■

Read the job advertisements on pages 66 and 67.

a. Find the key words that tell you what the requirements of each job are.

b. Divide the words into three lists, one referring to formal qualifications (degree, diploma, etc), one to experience and the third to personal characteristics.

c. Which is most important, qualifications or experience?

d. What do each of the words or phrases in the personal characteristics column mean?

e. Are there any general characteristics that all employers seem to be looking for?

f. How would you show that you possessed these characteristics?

■ TASK 2 ■

In groups of three, choose one of the advertisements. The three of you are going to interview applicants for the job.

a. Draw up a list of questions that you will ask each applicant, based on the requirements stated in the advertisement.

b. How would you expect the applicants to answer your questions?

■ TASK 3 ■

As a class, choose one of the advertisements. Three pairs will be interviewers, the rest of the class will be applicants for the job selected.

a. Interviewers: Prepare the questions that you will ask.

b. Applicants: Prepare a short curriculum vitae relating to the job.

Each pair of interviewers will interview several applicants, select the successful applicant and compare their choice with that of other interviewing teams, giving reasons for their choice.

■ TASK 4 ■

What characteristics do Chinese managers and directors value in their subordinates?

What are the characteristics valued by Australian employers?

Draw up a list of each and explain to your teacher how the two systems differ.

■ TASK 5 ■

Go through the job advertisements in one of the Saturday papers and find a job that you are qualified for. (Do not worry about your English level.)

a. Write out your curriculum vitae, remembering the qualifications specified in the advertisement.

b. What questions do you think the interviewers might ask you if you were interviewed for this job?

c. How would you answer them?

■ TASK 6 ■

Jiang Anshi applied for a job as a computer programmer in a large computing company. As he was very well qualified in computing and had extensive experience, he thought that he had a very good chance of getting the job. He was interviewed by three people who started out by asking him questions about his qualifications and experience. He answered confidently.

Suddenly, however, one of the interviewers asked him whether he could work in a team. Jiang Anshi was rather surprised at the question but said 'Yes'. He was then asked why he was interested in this particular job. He explained that the job was very suitable for him as he had done similar work before. He also explained that the salary was better than the salary he was currently receiving. Finally, he was asked if he himself had any questions. He did not.

Jiang Anshi left the interview feeling that he had done well. However, he did not get the job and later found out that the successful applicant had less experience than he had.

Why do you think Jiang Anshi didn't get the job?

■ TASK 7 ■

A friend has just arrived from China and is about to start looking for a job.

What advice would you give him?

■ TASK 8 ■

What information does an employer expect to find in a curriculum vitae?

What should a good curriculum vitae contain? Make a list.

Below is a poorly written curriculum vitae.

Read the biography of Li Anshi on the next page and rewrite his curriculum vitae more fully. Remember to pay attention to presentation.

CURRICULUM VITAE

Name:	Li Anshi
Age:	31
Address:	29 Smith St, Newville
Sex:	Male
Telephone:	123456789
Nationality:	Chinese

Education: Donghua Primary School 7   1976 – 2 1983
                    Sichuan Secondary School 2   1983 – 2 1987
                    Shanghai Technical College 7   1991 – 9 1995

Subject major: Electronics

Qualification: Diploma of Electronics

Experience:

    POSITION: Electronic Technician
    EMPLOYER: Shanghai University
    TIME: 9 years
    MAIN DUTIES: Assembly, maintenance and repair of equipment
    POSITION: Technician
    EMPLOYER: Austral Cable Company
    TIME: 18 months
    MAIN DUTIES: Maintenance and repair of equipment

Interests: Shanghai Electronics Association, repairing TVs and radios

References: Senior Engineer Deng Yaobang
                    Director of Technical Laboratory
                    University of Shanghai
                    Shanghai, China

                    John Smith
                    Personnel Officer
                    Austral Cable Company
                    Newville NSW 2999

TASK 8 continued

Below is a biography of Li Anshi. Use the information in this biography together with the information above to rewrite his curriculum vitae.

Li Anshi was born in Shanghai on 3 September 1968. He graduated from the Sichuan Secondary School in 1987 and immediately joined the People's Liberation Army where he trained as a technician. He remained in the army until mid-1991, working on the maintenance and repair of radio equipment.

In 1991 he resigned from the army and took a position in the Technical Department of Shanghai University. He worked there until 1999. At the beginning his work consisted of the maintenance and repair of the university's technical equipment. However, he then joined a team that was working on automatic control mechanisms for silk looms. The technology developed by the team was incorporated in a new range of high-speed, high-quality silk looms which were sold both in China and internationally.

Li Anshi then developed a computerised electronic timing device and an automatic feeding system for use in silk dyeing. The system was also rapidly adopted in Chinese silk mills. At the same time, he was responsible for directing the work of several technicians in his department.

In 1999 Li Anshi resigned from his job and came to Australia. He enrolled in a Master of Science degree in advanced automation techniques at the University of Science and Technology. At the same time, he also took a part-time job repairing electronic equipment in the Austral Cable Company.

Li Anshi has now been in Australia for two years.

Housing

Until the mid-1990s, housing in Chinese cities was controlled and distributed largely by work units. Few people owned their own homes and there was virtually no market in either buying or renting property. However, with reform of the SOEs has come the introduction of a market in housing which has had a major effect especially in big cities such as Beijing, Tianjin, Shanghai and in the southern province of Guangdong. Workers living in housing provided by work units have been encouraged to buy their flats at subsidised prices, and housing loans have been made available in order to facilitate this development. This is resulting in the creation of a large class of urban dwellers who are property owners.

In the few older style apartments owned by work units, rent remains cheap in comparison to wages, although the government is making a concerted effort to raise rents to full market value. Full market value is charged in the increasingly numerous apartment blocks built for the usually young and upwardly mobile middle class.

Large-scale private development of apartments and apartment blocks has taken place. This has resulted in the wholesale clearance of old housing in cities such as Beijing and Shanghai. In Beijing many of the old courtyard houses which gave the city its character have been destroyed and their mainly working class population re-housed in apartment blocks far from the city centre. In their place are modern and anonymous multistorey towers catering for a younger and wealthier clientele. Similar developments have taken place in many places, turning Chinese cities into clones of modern cities around the world.

Many peasant families living near large cities or close to major transport routes have also benefited from the prosperity that comes from a ready market for their produce, and have invested their earnings in substantial houses that witness their new found wealth.

The result of these developments is that living space has been increased. The average flat now consists of three rooms plus a kitchen and a bathroom. This is usually occupied by a husband and wife, their child and often one or more grandparents. House size is described in square metres rather than by number of bedrooms.

The fact that most people live in apartments has several consequences. Firstly, relations with neighbours are likely to be very close. It would be very difficult, and would be considered unnatural, not to know neighbours well. (This does not of course mean that relations will necessarily be good!) Everybody tends to know what everyone else is doing and if a family has visitors, everyone is likely to know. The exception to this is the southern coastal area, where people tend to be more protective of their privacy.

A second consequence is that family life tends to spill out onto the streets, especially during warm weather and in older areas. Preparation of food is frequently done outside on the street, as is the washing and drying of clothes. Old people sit outside their front doors, chatting and playing with their grandchildren, or play cards under street lights. Upon moving to Australia, many people miss this type of close-knit community and find life here lonely and drab.

However, people do not have to move overseas to experience this loss of community. One of the major criticisms levelled against the high rise blocks on city outskirts that house workers relocated from more central areas is that the outdoor life that they have enjoyed all their lives is greatly reduced, if not altogether impossible.

It is customary, when guests come to visit, to apologise for the simple and cramped nature of the home. This apology is given regardless of the actual state of the home – it is said equally of a mansion and a hovel – and is a polite convention not meant to be taken at face value.

In looking for an Australian home, many Chinese tend to prefer modern houses to older-style houses. The high prices fetched by inner-city housing often puzzle Australians!

Classroom Tasks

■ TASK 1 ■

Complete the table below for yourself, then ask an Australian to help you with the Australian figures.

Every month, how much is spent on each of the following?

	China		Australia	
	Amount	% of monthly income	Amount	% of monthly income
Rent				
Electricity				
Gas				
Food				
Transport				

a. Are there any differences in costs between Australia and China?

b. What is the most expensive aspect of living in China?

c. What is the most expensive aspect of living in Australia?

■ TASK 2 ■

Ma Jiaju has been living in a Melbourne suburb for five months, but he does not like the area very much and is thinking about moving. He asked his friend Peter for advice.

Peter asked why he wanted to move, and Ma Jiaju explained that his neighbours were racist and didn't like Chinese. Peter asked why he thought they were racist. Ma Jiaju replied that although he had lived in the area for five months, his neighbours had never spoken to him.

a. Is Ma Jiaju correct in his interpretation?

b. If you were Peter, what advice would you give Ma Jiaju?

■ TASK 3 ■

Tom and Jenny Carter are an Australian couple planning to buy a house. Zhang Songling and Lin Zhaohua, originally from China but now living in Australia, are also planning to buy a house. Both couples have good jobs and as yet have no children.

Below are brief descriptions of three houses. Each costs approximately the same and each is conveniently located.

Which house do you think the Australian couple would choose and which would the Chinese couple choose? Why?

List the advantages of each house:

■ from an Australian point of view

■ from a Chinese point of view.

Are there any differences in attitude about houses?

House A

This house is about 90 years old but is in excellent condition. It has recently been renovated, but the old fireplaces and small wooden windows have been preserved. It has two bedrooms, a living room and a dining room, and is situated close to the city centre in quite a densely populated area.

House B

This house is a very new townhouse. It features large windows with aluminium frames and looks very modern. It has two bedrooms, a living room and a dining room, and like house A is situated close to the city in a densely populated area.

House C

This house is about ten years old and is a typical suburban house about half an hour's train ride from the city centre. It has three bedrooms, a living room and a dining room, and is set in a garden.

Shopping

As with almost every other aspect of life in China, shopping has changed enormously over the last decade. In the large cities and generally in the rapidly developing coastal areas huge new department stores and shopping malls offer a range of goods every bit as wide as that available in Australia, Europe or America. Supermarkets sell both local and imported groceries and other essentials. The most important difference between China and most English speaking countries is the widespread existence of markets selling food and clothes. Bargaining is possible not only in these markets, but also in most small shops, and sometimes even in department stores.

Shops are open seven days a week, with Sunday being the busiest day. Most stores open between nine and ten in the morning and close around nine at night. Food markets, however, open at about four in the morning and are at their busiest before eight. Food is extremely expensive in comparison to income; the average family would spend at least 50 per cent of the combined family income on it.

Shopping for food is done on a daily basis, usually in the local market close to home. There is a widespread perception that fresh food is best, and a marked reluctance to store food for long. Most people also prefer to buy live fish and chickens to ensure freshness.

Both men and women do the shopping, depending usually on work commitments and convenience.

Service encounters

The way in which customers and shop assistants interact varies with the type of shop involved. Many modern department stores and shops now follow the pattern common in shops in English speaking countries, but others follow the traditional pattern. This traditional pattern involves the customer initiating the interaction by attracting the shop assistant's attention. The shop assistant does not usually accept payment for goods; rather, payment is made at a separate counter and two receipts issued, one retained by the customer and the second given to the shop assistant in return for the goods.

Multiple service is common. A shop assistant will serve several people at once, for example, by answering a query from one person, displaying merchandise to a second and finalising a sale with a third. Queuing for service is not common. A person with a rapid transaction to complete will expect to be served before or at the same time as someone who needs more time. It is certainly not expected that one transaction should be completed before another is begun.

As it is the shop assistant's duty to serve, politeness markers such as 'please' and 'thank you' are not used. Their use would in fact be considered excessive and even obsequious. Nor are requests marked for politeness; typical requests can be translated as follows:

'Give me ...'
'I want ...'

When translated into English, such requests tend to sound rather brusque. Conversely, English forms of request may be regarded as excessively polite.

Misunderstandings caused by differences in the way that service encounters are carried out are very common. Firstly, the difference in who initiates a transaction often results in misunderstanding. It is not uncommon for an English speaking customer to wait at the counter for the shop assistant to offer assistance while the shop assistant chats unconcernedly away with a colleague as she waits for the customer to call her over. In this situation, the English speaker often gets impatient and shows this by calling for assistance with an edge of annoyance in her voice. The shop assistant hears this edge, but does not understand the reason for it. She may decide that here is another example of an arrogant and possibly racist foreigner, which causes her to serve the customer somewhat brusquely. Things can escalate from there, and both customer and shop assistant may draw conclusions which are in fact totally unwarranted.

The situation is compounded by the differences in the language used to request items: as pointed out above, the Chinese lack of politeness markers may sound impolite to an English speaker, while that same speaker's use of such markers may sound obsequious to a Chinese speaker.

Finally, differences in the number of people that a shop assistant can serve at one time also has the potential to create negative impressions. Many English speakers feel that they are slighted if the assistant breaks off serving them to assist someone else. At the same time, many Chinese feel that they are being discriminated against when an English speaking assistant refuses to serve them until they have finished serving the previous client.

In all these cases, an understanding of the operating rules is usually enough to solve the problem.

Classroom Tasks

■ TASK 1 ■

Qin Guojun went into a post office to post a letter. There were already three other people at the counter and all of them had several letters and parcels to post. As he only wanted to buy a stamp, Qin Guojun walked up to the counter and asked for an ordinary stamp. The assistant told him to wait and refused to serve him while she continued to serve the other customers in the line.

Why didn't the assistant help Qin Guojun?

■ TASK 2 ■

Mary Watson wanted to buy a scarf as a souvenir of her trip to Shanghai. She saw a scarf she liked in a shop and decided to buy it. There were few other people in the shop and the shop assistants were not busy, but they didn't seem to notice her. Finally she called out 'Excuse me' and an assistant came to serve her. However, while she was looking at the scarf, the assistant began serving someone else. Mary decided to buy the scarf and waited while the assistant served the other customer. Then while the assistant was wrapping up the scarf she paused to answer another customer's question. Mary was extremely angry and left the store without buying the scarf.

Why didn't Mary buy the scarf?

■ TASK 3 ■

This research project is designed to help you observe how Australians behave in shops.

You should do this project with a partner and prepare your report together.

Together with your partner, go into a sandwich shop which has several customers in it. Stand at the back of the shop, watch what people do and listen to what they say. Make notes. Try and answer the following questions:

a. How many people does the assistant serve at one time?

b. How does she choose who to serve next?

c. Who speaks first, the assistant or the customer?

d. How do the customers order what they want? Note at least three different ways of ordering.

e. What does the assistant say?

f. Does anyone say 'Please' or 'Thank you'? When do they say it?

When you have completed your observations, go back to your class and prepare a report on your findings.

a. How do your findings compare with the findings of other pairs?

b. How does buying in an Australian shop compare with buying in China?

NB: It may help if you speak to the shopkeeper first (preferably early in the morning when there aren't so many customers) and ask his or her permission to observe.

Health

Health care in Chinese cities is based round the hospital and supplemented by a network of local clinics. It used to be free to all those working for state-owned companies and enterprises, and family members of employees enjoyed subsidised care. However, the amount of money spent on health care has declined dramatically in recent years and free and subsidised care is largely a thing of the past. Most hospitals and clinics now charge for their services, usually by means of an up-front fee for each service. Health insurance is available, but it is expensive and limited to specific hospitals and nominated services. The result is that many poorer members of the community seek medical treatment only when they are seriously ill.

Seeing the doctor

As all doctors are based in hospitals or, to a lesser extent, in local clinics, a person would normally go straight to a hospital in the event of illness. In the cities, there is a strong preference for treatment in a hospital rather than a clinic, and both in the cities and in the countryside most would not go to the hospital for minor or familiar illnesses but would buy the appropriate medication from a local pharmacy.

In the cities, almost all hospitals have departments of both Chinese traditional medicine and western medicine. Many people rely on traditional medicine for minor illnesses and turn to western medicine for serious complaints. Many country dwellers tend to distrust western medicine except in emergencies.

Having seen the doctor, patients may collect the prescribed medicine from the pharmacy attached to the hospital. However, prices at hospital pharmacies tend to be much more expensive than prices elsewhere. This is because hospitals are limited in the fees that they can charge for medical and nursing services, and so are forced to charge high prices for use of facilities and for medications.

Talking about health

Health and how to retain it and restore it constitutes a popular topic of conversation for old and retired people, and discussions of the properties of various medicines and folk remedies are very common.

In other sections of the population, concern with a healthy lifestyle is also evident. This manifests itself in several ways. Firstly, great care tends to be taken with food, especially among the middle-aged. Nobody ever drinks unboiled water and all fruit and vegetables are peeled before being eaten. The sight of Australians drinking water straight from the tap and eating unpeeled apples can be unnerving to new arrivals!

At work, this concern reflects itself in the provision of boiled water. Every office is invariably supplied with thermoses of boiled water and this is regarded as a basic necessity. In Australia, the failure in particular of schools and universities to make such provision can be seen as evidence either of incompetence or neglect of the most basic consideration of human welfare.

Concern with the maintenance of health is also reflected in attitudes to clothing. In the north, where winters are very cold, people wear heavy, padded clothing and the failure to dress properly is often cited as a cause of ill health. 'Wear more clothes' is a frequently heard expression of concern and friendship. Babies and small children in particular are bundled up to a much greater extent than would be the case in Australia.

Exercise is popular, especially among young men and older people. Young men tend to focus on martial arts and jogging, while older people favour *tai chi chuan* and related exercises. Tai Chi is, in general, regarded as an old people's sport in much the same way as lawn bowls is regarded in Australia.

Attitudes to smoking are similar to the attitudes prevailing in Australia in the 1940s and 1950s. Most workers and many intellectuals smoke, though students tend not to because of the expense. Women who smoke are comparatively rare, but an increasing number of trendy middle-class women are taking up the habit.

Being sick

When someone is sick, either in hospital or at home, it is usual for their friends to visit them. Not to visit would usually be taken to indicate a lack of concern for a friend's wellbeing and therefore a lack of true friendship. Presents of fruit are often given, though in the Shanghai region, apples are avoided as in Shanghai dialect the word for apple sounds the same as 'to die of an illness'!

Classroom Tasks

■ TASK 1 ■

When you are sick, what do you do in China? How does it compare with what people do in Australia?

Write a short brochure, comparing how to see a doctor and where to buy medicine in China and in Australia, that would be useful for foreign students going to study in China.

Getting around

Bicycles

The most common means of getting around in China is the bicycle. Almost everyone can and does ride almost everywhere. Most families have one bicycle, many have one for each family member. Maintenance costs are low and most repairs that cannot be done by the owner can be done by one of the bicycle-repair men who set up shop beside the road.

Bicycle theft is a major problem, so people are careful to lock up their bicycles whenever they are left on the street.

Traffic rules

Traffic in China drives on the right-hand side of the road. Road rules are similar to those in Australia. However, many people, especially young men, tend to ride or drive very fast and to ignore other road users. They are therefore unprepared for Australian roads and for the unforgiving driving style of most Australian drivers. On the other hand, many Chinese are impressed by the fact that in Australia, drivers stop to allow pedestrians to cross the road, something that rarely happens in China.

Cars and taxis

The number of private cars on Chinese roads has increased astronomically over the last decade. While still the preserve of the relatively wealthy, they are no longer the preserve of the elite. The number of motorbikes and scooters has also increased dramatically, and as a result, road congestion and air pollution have both increased. The government attempts to regulate ownership by mandating an extremely thorough, lengthy and costly process to obtain a licence and by imposing a range of taxes. Restrictions on the availability of motorbikes and scooters are being considered, as these are considered to be considerably more polluting than cars.

The number of taxis has also increased dramatically, and these are normally reasonably priced and reliable.

Public transport

Within cities, the most common form of public transport is buses and trolleys. They provide a cheap, frequent and reliable service and very few areas are unserviced. Overcrowding is their main shortcoming and in certain cities this is an enormous problem. All bus stops are clearly marked with the route number and a schematic map of all stops on the route. Passengers pay a standard fare, regardless of the distance being travelled. As in Australia, most buses do not have conductors; fare collection is automated and in general exact change is necessary. It is not uncommon to see passengers who need change collecting fares from other passengers, calling out the amount they are depositing and the number of fares they are collecting as they do so.

In spite of (or perhaps because of!) the extreme overcrowding, queuing is very rare and getting on a bus often involves a great deal of pushing and shoving.

Intercity transport is provided by trains and by long-distance buses. Trains provide three classes of seats – hard seat, hard sleeper and soft seat or sleeper. Tickets, particularly sleeper tickets, are often difficult to buy and *guanxi* can be useful in obtaining them.

Air transport is increasingly available and is used mainly by business people and those working for large companies.

Directions and distances

Directions are normally given in terms of compass points rather than by using left and right. While maps of most large cities are available, they usually cover only the central city area and almost always omit the details of the networks of small alleys and streets where most people live. People therefore do not generally rely on maps when going to an unfamiliar area, but tend to take with them someone who already knows the area. Reading maps printed in English may therefore present some initial problems.

Classroom Tasks

■ **TASK 1** ■

How does transport in China differ from transport in Australia?

a. If you could introduce one change in the transportation system in your home town, what would that change be?

b. If you could introduce one change in the transportation system in Australia, what would it be?

■ **TASK 2** ■

In China, bicycles are the main means of private transportation. In Australia, cars are most important.

a. If Australians changed their cars to bicycles, what would the results be? Would you support such a change?

b. If Chinese changed their bicycles for cars, what would the results be? Would you support such a change?

CHAPTER ■ SIX

INTERACTING IN SOCIETY

An examination of the contents page of almost any modern English language textbook reveals the importance placed on language as a tool, as a means of doing things. Asking permission, apologising, greeting, leave-taking, agreeing and disagreeing are all functional descriptions of language. The linguistic realisations of these functions form the basis of much of general language teaching. However, such functions naturally occur within a context; that is, they are spoken in specific situations and these situations evoke in speaker and listener specific expectations. For example, when apologising, both speaker and listener have expectations about what actions warrant an apology and about what determines the depth of the apology. There are expectations relating to whether an apology will be accepted or rejected and how either the acceptance or rejection should be carried out. There may be certain physical gestures that accompany a verbal apology. All these are relevant in determining the actual linguistic realisation of the apology. When speaker and listener come from the same culture their expectations on these and other points are likely to be very similar. However, when the two are from different cultures, then the likelihood is that they will have different expectations regarding any or all of them. Inappropriate behaviour or miscommunication is likely to be the result. This chapter will attempt to indicate some of the assumptions that are associated with the functions most commonly occurring in basic English-language textbooks.

A word of warning is, however, appropriate at this stage. While it is true that the assumptions of the mother culture are likely to influence the student's use of English, it is also true that the student's perceptions of the new culture (in this case, of Australian culture) are important. Specifically, most Chinese believe as a general rule that English speakers are in any given circumstance more direct than Chinese. In speaking English, then, they may deliberately choose the most direct realisation of a given function in the mistaken belief that they are being culturally appropriate. Teachers need to spend time with their students exploring Australian assumptions related to the realisation of functions in specific situations.

Socialising

Greetings

The most common semiformal and formal greeting in Chinese can be roughly translated as 'How are you?' Like its English equivalent, it is usually reciprocal. When addressing superiors, it would be usual to replace the pronoun with the occupational title of the person addressed.

| Ni | hao | ma? |
| You | well | Question |

Laoshi	hao	ma?
Teacher	well	Question

A wide range of informal greetings is used between friends, including 'Where are you going?', 'Have you eaten?' and 'What have you bought?'. Such greetings do not require an accurate answer; the usual response to the first one, for example, being 'I'm going to buy something' or 'I'm going over there'. It is usual when meeting friends in public to stop and greet them. Many Chinese interpret as unfriendly the common Australian habit of greeting friends on the street with a smile and a brief word without stopping.

At the same time there are occasions when it is usual for an Australian to greet someone when a Chinese person might not. A common example of this lack of greeting is to be found in the workplace. Upon arriving at work, people frequently do not greet each other but simply get on with their work. A brief nod of the head may also be used. In such cases, it is common for the subordinate to greet the superior using his occupational title while the superior nods in reply. Such a greeting is also possible between students and teachers.

On formal occasions people tend to shake hands on greeting but, in informal situations involving friends, body contact is not usual. Many Chinese are shocked on first seeing Australian friends of opposite sexes kissing each other in greeting. Such public physical contact would be rare even between husband and wife after a period of separation and would certainly not occur between friends.

Classroom Tasks

■ TASK 1 ■

Following is part of a letter written by an Australian working in China to a friend. Read the extract and comment on the questions below.

> ... Well, I've been here in Tianjin for two months now and on the whole I'm enjoying it. My work is interesting and my colleagues are friendly and helpful. However, there are some things that I am finding a little difficult. For example, I don't like the way everyone watches you all the time. Every time I meet someone I know, they ask me where I am going. It makes me feel as if I have no privacy, I can't do anything without everyone knowing about it. I know that privacy isn't very important here, but it's still difficult to get used to.
>
> Apart from little things like that, everything is fine. Last Sunday I went ...

Why does the letter writer feel that he has no privacy?

Is the writer correct in his analysis? How would you explain the situation to him? Write a short letter explaining the Chinese point of view.

What differences have you noticed between the way Chinese greet each other and the way Australians greet each other?

Introducing

In formal situations, the superior or older person is introduced first. The family name is used together with the appropriate occupational title. In general, people avoid using the given names of older people or superiors. Shaking hands is usual in such situations. In informal situations, people may also be introduced using only the family name and they would then be addressed by that name plus a diminutive. Such a form of introduction would be used if the encounter were casual and not expected to result in further contact. A more formal introduction, still between friends but one that suggested the possibility of further contact, might use the full name. There is in many places, however, a reluctance to use, or even to mention, the full name in front of strangers. So, for example, senders often avoid writing their names on envelopes and people may hesitate before giving their name over the phone.

Classroom Tasks

■ TASK 1 ■

Divide the class into groups of four and give each group one of the cards below.

Each group role-plays two introductions between the people described on the cards. In the first case, the people involved are Australians; in the second case, Chinese.

After role-playing, students can explain the differences between the two in terms of:

■ body language

■ language.

Situations

a. You are in your mid-20s. Introduce a friend to your mother and father.

b. You are walking down the street with two friends. You see someone you know, though you don't know him well. You stop for a brief chat. How would you introduce him to your other two friends?

c. You are the production manager of a large factory. You are attending a conference with your deputy manager. You meet a similar manager and an engineer from another factory. How do you introduce each other?

d. You are in a cafe with two friends. Suddenly a close friend walks in. Introduce him or her to your other two friends.

e. A new person has started work in your section. Introduce him or her to the other people working in the section.

Naming

In Chapter 4, page 33, we explained that in Chinese the family name comes first and is followed by a given name which is usually composed of two characters. However, this given name is not used in the same way as it is in Australia; that is, it is not used as a term of address except in intimate circumstances. For this reason, and to avoid problems with pronunciation, many Chinese adopt English first names that can be safely used by English speakers. Unfortunately, some English speakers attempt to use the Chinese given name even when an English alternative is available in the mistaken belief that they are being culturally appropriate.

The option of not using a name at all is available in both English and Chinese, but in different circumstances. The paradigm case of this is in telephone conversations. When answering the telephone, Chinese people often do not state their own names. Instead, they may ask who is calling. The caller may then inquire for the person they want without revealing his or her own name. Of course the danger is that the refusal of either to give their name may result in a total breakdown of communication, which does in fact happen.

Australian teachers need to be aware that Chinese learners may be sensitive about their names, and use English names if possible. Failing that, they should use the family name, and a title, especially when dealing with older people.

Leave-taking

Most teachers who have invited their Chinese students home for a party or barbecue will be familiar with one aspect of Chinese leave-taking – when everyone leaves in a group at about ten o'clock! Chinese leave-takings may appear to Australians to be either rather abrupt or overly elaborate, depending on the relative status of the people involved.

The most common leave-taking formula between friends translates literally as 'I'll leave first'. It needs very little or no introduction and it is not expected that the person leaving would be urged to stay. Another common expression basically means that the person involved is busy and has other things to do.

As described above, people tend to arrive and leave in groups, especially in semi-formal situations where the people involved are not close friends. This is, of course, typically the case where Chinese are visiting Australians. Nor in general do people keep very late hours – eleven o'clock at night tends to be regarded as a late night.

It is common for the host to accompany his guests as they leave; to the bus stop, for example, or at least to where they had parked their bicycles (or cars).

In formal situations, people wait for the most senior person to leave. This also applies to the classroom situation, where students usually wait for their teacher to leave before they leave. In such situations, it is the senior person who initiates the leave-taking and he or she is usually shortly followed by all the other guests.

Classroom Tasks

■ TASK 1 ■

Read the following description of a situation where cross-cultural miscommunication occurs. What do you think caused the miscommunication?

Lin Fengsong had called in to see his friend Peter Rowe. However, Lin knew Peter was quite busy and did not want to disturb him, so after they had chatted for a while, Lin said, 'Well, I've got some business, I'll go now.' Peter accompanied him to his car and said goodbye. That evening, Peter told his wife about Lin's visit. He said, 'I don't know whether I said something wrong or if Lin was being rude. He just said he had some business and he went. I felt a bit embarrassed. I hope I didn't upset him.'

a. Was Lin Fengsong angry?

b. Why did Peter think he was angry?

c. What advice would you give Peter and Lin Fengsong so that they can avoid this situation in future?

■ TASK 2 ■

This project involves you listening to what Australians say when they take leave of each other.

To carry out the research, you will need to draw up a table like the one below. Two examples have been given to help you get started. While you are on the train, out shopping, or walking down the street, listen to what people say and fill in the table.

Your research should take about a week. When you have finished, you could compare your results with the results of others in your class.

Date	Place	Sex	Age	What they said
12 June	Train	1 M 1 F	30s 30s	See you tomorrow. See you.
12 June	Street	2 M 1 F	20s 20s	I'll give you a ring. Drive carefully.

Agreeing, disagreeing and expressing opinions

An Australian adviser involved in formulating policy on the future of Chinese students in Australia at the time of the Tiananmen massacre asked a prominent Chinese intellectual for his opinion.

The intellectual replied by summarising the experience of the Chinese students, explaining their motives for coming to Australia in the first place and the impact on their thinking both of events in China and the uncertainty of Australian government policy. The summary was an intelligent and carefully reasoned analysis of the situation and finished with a number of clearly stated proposals. The adviser, however, was wearing a faintly glazed expression by the end of the talk and later commented that he had had difficulty in picking up the thread of the argument being presented. He felt that the intellectual had not really thought out his case and that his ideas were vague and unorganised.

Clearly, something was interfering with communication. To find out what, we need to briefly examine certain aspects of English argument. When presenting a position in English, or making a demand, we usually state at the beginning what our opinion or demand is, and then outline the reasons for holding or making it. This convention is especially obvious in writing, where the introduction summarises the argument, the topic sentence of each paragraph outlines the direction of the argument and the conclusion confirms or modifies the argument and is specifically designed not to introduce any point that has not already been made in the body of the essay.

Now let us look at how the intellectual presented his position. He first outlined the background to the current situation, examining the reasons that Chinese students gave for coming to Australia. He then went over the changes in perception that had occurred among students as a result of both the Chinese and Australian governments' actions. Having established a shared basis of understanding, allowing his listener to follow his chain of reasoning, he then presented his recommendations. However, by this time, the Australian listener had already switched off. He was used to listening carefully to the opening of an argument and to taking from there a summary of the conclusion. This was then used as a standard for evaluating the arguments put forward in support of that conclusion. In listening to the Chinese speaker, he was unable to carry out this type of evaluation and so felt that the argument lacked focus and force.

Chinese argument on the other hand seeks to build a case that gradually unfolds, taking the listener through the speaker's steps so that the reasoning behind the conclusions is transparent, and speaker and listener arrive at the same conclusion together. If Australians tend to find Chinese argument unfocused, Chinese often consider the Australian style repetitive. They tend to ignore later parts of an argument, feeling that as they already know the conclusion, further information is redundant.

This pattern of verbal argument is also found in writing. Introductions that present the main line of argument and sketch in the conclusion are largely absent in Chinese writing. Topic sentences in each paragraph are also rarely present. A Chinese introduction is more likely to outline aspects of the background to the problem, especially aspects of the historical background. It may therefore appear irrelevant to an Australian reader.

Another case illustrates a further difference in the organisation of information in an argument. This case concerns a joint venture in Beijing, an undertaking involving Chinese and Australian partners. Australian-recruited specialists were working together with Chinese specialists in establishing the joint venture. One of the Australians, though skilled in his area of responsibility, was extremely unhappy with many of the organisational aspects of the project and made constant, and extremely vocal criticisms of the Chinese leadership. He also shocked this leadership, who were socially and politically conservative, by his informal dress and his habit of flirting with the girls involved in the project. At the half-yearly management meeting, an extremely important meeting, the subject of this project member was raised, but not directly. The Chinese head-of-project began by praising the work of all people involved in the project. He spoke at length about the difficulties overcome and the enormous contributions made and sacrifices endured by the Australian participants. He enumerated the successes achieved. Only right at the end of his speech did he comment on the importance of careful selection of project members, stressing the importance of respecting others' customs and working for the common good. At no stage was the name of the offending party mentioned, but he expected that from the outset the message was quite clear.

This case illustrates an important point. The Chinese leadership was registering its disapproval of the selection procedures used by the Australian company, but did not immediately raise this issue. First, the overall direction of the project and the contribution of other project members were favourably reviewed and then the point of discontent and disagreement was raised indirectly. In this case, the Australian participants understood the implied message. This is not always the case, especially as attention to the opening section of the speech would tend to suggest to an Australian that all was well.

Another case involving the same joint venture casts further light on the areas of agreeing, disagreeing and expressing opinions. The Australian side of this project had provided most of the material and equipment necessary to start the plant, including a car. The use of this car became the focus of an ongoing battle that was regularly raised at each six-monthly management meeting. The Australians claimed that the car had been provided for project use during working hours and for private use by Australian project members outside office hours. They claimed that this implied Australian team members should be able to drive it. The Chinese felt that the car should only be driven by authorised Chinese drivers, which effectively limited its use by Australians but increased its use by senior Chinese project members. The point of contention was the registration. The car was first provided with a registration that precluded it being driven by Australian project members. The Australians' aim was to change this registration. The Chinese were apologetic – it could not legally be done. The Australians cited the Memorandum of Understanding that formed the legal basis of the project; they cited Chinese law and precedent. All concurred that it was possible. The Chinese authorities countered with a number of practical difficulties, but conceded that the Australians had the right to drive the car and promised to look into the matter.

Six months later nothing had changed. The matter was again raised at the six-monthly meeting; the right of the Australians to drive the car was again acknowledged, difficulties again mentioned and action again promised. Six months later, nothing had changed.

There are two significant points to note about this case. The first is that at no stage did the Chinese authorities refuse the Australian request. Rather, they promised an investigation but did nothing. The second is that both sides considered the other side not only unreasonable but also unreliable. The Australians considered that they had a legal right on their side and that this legal right had been acknowledged. This being the case, they could not see any reason for further delay. The Chinese pointed out the practical difficulties involved and considered that by doing so they had indicated the impossibility of complying with the Australians' request. They regarded their commitment to 'look into it' as a way of allowing the Australians to withdraw gracefully, not as a commitment to solving the problem. They failed to understand the importance the Australians attached to the legal position, while the Australians failed to understand the implications of the Chinese promise of action.

The next time you attend a meeting, select an item on the agenda and note the following:

Organisation of argument

What was the purpose of the item – for example, reporting, discussing, other?

How was the topic introduced?

At what point was the course of action to be followed introduced?

When were justifications for the course of action introduced?

Organisation of discussion

How was discussion initiated?

Who contributed to the discussion?

How were contributors to the discussion selected?

Did anyone dominate the discussion? If so, what allowed him or her to do so?

Presenting opinions

Were dissenting opinions presented? If so, how were they introduced?

If not, why not?

Was a conclusion reached? If so was it by consensus, by vote or in some other way?

What conclusions can you draw about Australian patterns of discussion and debate?

If different conventions regarding the organisation of information cause communication breakdown, there are also several other aspects of presenting a position that similarly result in problems. The first of these concerns the possibility of expressing an opinion at all. Many teachers believe that Chinese are reluctant to express individual opinions, and that they are as a result 'passive'. Even a cursory glance at the history of 20th-century China reveals that Chinese have been conspicuously ready to express their opinions in the most forceful of ways. There are, however, a number of situations where it would not be considered appropriate to express an opinion. These situations usually involve significant differences in either the status or the age of participants. So, for example, it would be unusual for subordinates to advance personal opinions in the presence of a superior, and extremely unusual to advance an opinion contradicting that of a superior in public. Such an action would be seen as a direct attack on the superior and a deliberate attempt to undermine his or her position.

Rather, subordinates are expected to support their superior's position, regardless of their personal feelings about the matter. In the same way, students would not, in general, disagree with their teacher, especially in high school and in the early years of university studies. A student's task is to absorb what the teacher has to give so as to establish a basis for later (possibly critical) development.

When talking to people of roughly equal status and age, however, opinions are advanced and defended forcefully and often more directly than would be the case in Australia. This may give rise to problems in certain situations involving Chinese and Australians. For example, Australians tend to stress equality as a value in their inter-actions with others. If this claim to equality is acknowledged and recognised by a Chinese, it may result in the Chinese then expressing him or herself in a way that is regarded by an Australian as unduly pushy or forceful.

Another aspect of expressing opinions that is of relevance to teachers with Chinese students relates to topic choice. Topics that are either controversial or of great com-munity interest in one culture are not necessarily so in another culture. An example that springs readily to mind is the death penalty. Most Chinese would have very little quarrel with the death penalty for certain types of crime and therefore do not find very much to say if asked to debate it.

> Look at the topics set for discussion in any English language teaching textbook.
>
> Are the topics likely to interest Chinese students?
>
> Divide the topics into two groups according to whether you think Chinese students would or would not be interested in discussing them.
>
> Present the same list to a class of Chinese students and ask them to do the same.
>
> Compare their choice with your own predictions.

Classroom Tasks

■ TASK 1 ■

Read the following case study. What advice would you give Wu Weimin?

> Wu Weimin had just started work for an Australian company that had extensive business commitments in China. A large part of his work concerned advising his Australian colleagues on Chinese business practices. This involved writing reports and recommendations, and addressing meetings. As he was very anxious to succeed, Wu Weimin always researched his topics thoroughly and tried to make his presentations as clear as possible. However, he gradually became aware that something was wrong. It often seemed that nobody listened to him and his advice was usually ignored. When he spoke at meetings, he felt that people were impatient and uninterested in what he had to say. He got more and more unhappy and began to feel that his colleagues were not interested in his opinions because he was Chinese. This, he thought, was racism.

The company had a policy of annual review, which meant that every staff member met with the managing director once a year to discuss his or her progress. When the time came for Wu Weimin's review, the managing director gave him a copy of the company's assessment of his performance. The assessment praised his hard work, but made the following, very serious, criticisms:

i.   When speaking at meetings, arguments often unfocused, speeches lacking clear direction.

ii.   Written reports contain too much irrelevant material.

iii. In both speaking and writing, material poorly organised, with important recommendations often appearing only at the end of the report.

iv.   Often appears uncertain about points he wants to make.

Wu Weimin was shocked by these criticisms. He could not understand why they had been made and he was not sure what to do about them.

Why do you think the company criticised Wu Weimin in this way?

What would you advise him to do:

■ in the interview itself

■ in his future work, so as to avoid such criticism in future?

■ TASK 2 ■

By now, you must be familiar with the use of introductions, topic sentences and conclusions in formal English writing.

a. Does Chinese use a similar system of organising information?

b. Describe how you would write a report or essay in Chinese.

c. What are the advantages and disadvantages of each system? List them on a sheet of paper, then compare your list with those of other students in the class.

■ TASK 3 ■

Take any current affairs program on television and video a segment involving an interview.

Answer the following questions:

a. Who are the participants?

b. What topic is being discussed?

c. Is disagreement stated directly or indirectly?

d. Note down three expressions used to indicate agreement.

e. Note down three expressions used to indicate:

- direct disagreement

- indirect disagreement.

Choose one of the speakers:

a. What course of action does he or she support?

b. What does he or she talk about first:

- What he/she wants to do

  or

- Why he/she wants to do it?

Do you agree or disagree with his arguments? Why?

Expressing emotions and feelings

The open expression of strong emotions is not encouraged in Chinese culture. This, of course, does not mean that emotions are not expressed, but that in general the expression of emotions, particularly negative emotions such as anger, impatience and grief, is restrained. People who do express their anger and frustration or even their exuberance too forcefully tend to be regarded as lacking in education – 'having a low cultural level' as the Chinese would put it. They are perceived as being pushy, demanding and overbearing.

The ways in which emotions are expressed are governed by the concept of 'inner' and 'outer' relationships. This concept is discussed more fully in Chapter 7, page 121, but in brief, inner relationships are close relationships, while outer relationships are distant. The relationship between family members is an inner relationship, as is the relationship between close friends. Relationships with colleagues are also inner relationships, though less so than those with family. An outer relationship, on the other hand, is basically no relationship at all. The relationship between a group of people waiting for a bus, or that between people on the street, is an outer relationship. Inner relationships are characterised by politeness and consideration for others, while outer relations are not. With regard to the expression of emotions, this means that restraint is expected in inner relationships, but not in outer relationships. For example, a person would not normally display anger towards people with whom he or she shared an inner relationship, but would not be so reticent when only outer relationships were involved.

The boundary between inner and outer is to a certain extent fluid and open to negotiation: people may start as acquaintances with an outer relationship and move slowly towards an increasingly inner relationship as the acquaintance ripens into friendship.

If subject to stress, a relationship may be redefined, shifting rapidly from inner to outer. In other words, people may restrain their emotions, especially anger and frustration, up to a certain point. Once that point is reached there may be a rapid transition from seeming calm to forceful expressions of anger or discontent. This may appear to an Australian as an unwarranted escalation as it contrasts to the more gradual build-up common in Australia. Australians are also not likely to recognise the change in relationship that is signalled by anger, and may be unprepared for the lasting consequences that may eventuate.

One result of the suppression of strong emotions is that smiling, laughing and giggling are used to mask more negative emotions. This may tend to mislead Australians. An illustration of this occurred in a language school. A Chinese student was rebuked for walking straight into the director's office without knocking. The student's reaction was to laugh. The teacher felt that she was being laughed at and became extremely angry, much to the amazement of the student who was not sure why she had been criticised in the first place and had absolutely no idea what had provoked the anger. Her laughter was an expression of embarrassment.

Because laughter can be used to cover anger or frustration, Australians may be unaware of the underlying anger, imagining from the laughter that all is well. They may then be shocked if the Chinese, finding that politeness is getting them nowhere, actually does show anger.

Public displays of affection are in general viewed very negatively, and many Chinese are shocked to see Australian couples kissing in public.

The Australian attitude that emotions should not be bottled up but should be expressed and even shared is not an attitude accepted by Chinese and is one that is not easily understood, particularly by people of the older generation.

Classroom Tasks

■ TASK 1 ■

Read the following case study and explain what has gone wrong.

What would you advise the two participants to do in future?

> Hu Zuoping had just started work in a new company. It was morning tea time and he was sitting in the tearoom smoking a cigarette. Suddenly one of his workmates came in and angrily pointed to a 'No smoking' sign. Hu Zuoping was very embarrassed. He laughed and put his cigarette out. However, this did not seem to satisfy the man, who started to talk rapidly and angrily. Hoping to calm him down, Hu Zuoping smiled and apologised, trying to explain that he had not noticed the sign. However, the man got even more angry. Finally, another worker came into the room and calmed him down, but as the first man left, he still looked angrily at Hu Zuoping. Hu Zuoping sighed; he knew he had made a bad start, but still didn't understand why.

■ TASK 2 ■

Emotions and feelings are often associated with colours.

Fill in the table below and compare the possible meaning of colours in Australian and Chinese culture.

The first one about Australia is done for you.

Colour	Meaning in Chinese culture	Meaning in Australian culture
Yellow		Cowardice
Red		
Blue		
Black		
White		
Green		
Purple		

Complimenting

I vividly remember going to visit a close Chinese friend whom I hadn't seen for several years. I walked into the house and her mother greeted me with a broad smile and told me I'd got fat. Knowing that she was being both friendly and polite in complimenting me like that did not comfort me at all!

Complimenting is an area where differences between Chinese and English usage are complicated by widespread misapprehensions. In regard to the differences, there are several areas where a compliment in one language becomes an extremely rude statement in the other. Examples are age and appearance. Age becomes an appropriate subject for compliment once a person is over about 60 in China. In Australia a similar situation only exists when a person nears 100 and, in general, a 60-year-old would take exception to being publicly classified as old.

On the other hand, complimenting a woman on her appearance is widely practised in Australia but has an almost exclusively sexual connotation in China. In general, however, it is not so much the content of complimentary remarks that differ as the reactions to them. In English, a person usually responds to a compliment by denying it:

Oh, I just threw whatever was in the fridge into the pot.

By pointing out limitations or redirecting credit:

My mother taught me how to make it.

Or by accepting it:

Thank you. I'm glad you like it.

In Chinese, the third alternative is not usually available. Responses to compliments are usually self-deprecating, so that a woman who is complimented on her cooking may well reply:

Oh, it was far from being a good dish.

The fact that in English it is possible under certain circumstances to accept a compliment, however, gives rise to a major and widespread misapprehension among Chinese students; that all compliments are invariably accepted in English. When this strategy is implemented in English by Chinese speakers, they tend to sound pushy and big-noting.

Differences in the content of compliments also means that people are often unsure of how to reply to a compliment, especially when they are not sure of the meaning behind it (as might be the case, for example, when a woman is complimented on her appearance).

> How can teachers prevent over-generalisation of cultural rules?
>
> Are there any advantages in this over-generalisation?
>
> How does over-generalisation relate to stereotyping?

Classroom Tasks

■ TASK 1 ■

Mr John Carr was part of a tourist group visiting the Great Wall. He was a little older than most of the others in the party, but was one of the most energetic of the group. After he had climbed up to two of the watchtowers in the time most people took to reach one, his guide, a young woman, complimented him on his age and fitness. While Mr Carr did not reply, it was obvious that he was not happy.

If you were a guide, what would you say to Mr Carr?

■ TASK 2 ■

How do people compliment each other in Chinese?

In groups, write down as many situations as you can think of where people would compliment each other.

Explain what people say and how they reply. Now do the same for English.

Explain the Chinese situation to your teacher and ask for her comments on your explanation of Australian customs.

■ TASK 3 ■

How does your teacher compliment students?

List the different compliments she gives over the next week.

Are your Australian teacher's compliments the same as a Chinese teacher's compliments?

At the end of the week, present a short talk to the class comparing the use of compliments by Chinese and Australian teachers. Make sure your teacher understands the Chinese situation.

Asking for permission

During the course of a survey on teacher attitudes to Chinese students and their problems, one complaint was raised again and again. It went like this:

The main problem is that students don't really want to study. I don't mind if they're working, I can understand that, but usually that's not the problem. They come up to you and say 'I have to help my friend tomorrow, so I can't come to school'. Any excuse to get out of school. And they never ask. They just tell you.

There are two problems involved here. The first relates to perceptions of student attitudes to class, perceptions that are in part formed by student reasons for not coming to class. The second relates to the actual form of words used. Is the teacher justified in drawing the conclusion that is drawn in the above example?

Socially acceptable reasons for doing or not doing something vary from culture to culture and are usually linked to key community attitudes. In China, the obligation to help family members and friends is a key attitude, so one of the most common reasons offered for absence is precisely that given above. Variations include taking relatives to hospital and meeting friends at the airport or train station. In Australian culture, the demands of family and especially of friends are, in general, ranked below those of work and so these types of excuses are not acceptable. As with the teacher quoted above, they tend to be taken as evidence of lack of commitment and serious purpose.

The second problem in the above situation relates to the actual words used. Students appear to inform rather than request. In Chinese the request is often implicit and lies in the reasons given for a course of action. Thus if, for example, a worker tells his supervisor that his relatives are arriving tomorrow, the supervisor understands the implicit request for the day off. When the request is spelled out, it is more usual to use a form that, directly translated, appears to inform rather than request.

In addition to these differences, there are many occasions when it is not necessary to seek permission in Chinese culture. These include sitting down at a table when some seats are already occupied, opening windows and smoking.

For what activities do Australians usually have to seek permission?

What types of reasons form socially acceptable justifications for these actions?

Are there any situations where we have to seek permission but don't have to justify our actions?

Classroom Tasks

■ TASK 1 ■

Below are several situations in which one person has to ask another for permission to do something.

With a partner, role-play one of these situations. Your teacher will comment on the appropriateness of what you say.

a. You work in a city office and you can't come to work tomorrow. Ask your supervisor for the day off.

b. You go into a coffee shop for a cup of coffee, but unfortunately there are no free tables. However, a young woman is sitting alone at a table with one spare seat.

c. You are a factory worker and your sister is arriving at the airport tomorrow. You want to meet her. Ask the supervisor for the day off.

d. You are sitting in a waiting room with several other people, waiting for your long-distance train. You want to smoke. The area is a smoking area.

e. You are studying English and you want to leave class half an hour early every day. Ask your teacher for permission.

■ TASK 2 ■

You have to take a day off work to attend to some urgent personal business. What reasons would you give your superior for taking time off work:

■ in Australia

■ in China?

Are there any reasons that are acceptable in China but are not acceptable in Australia? What about the reverse situation: are there reasons that are acceptable in Australia but not in China?

Make a list of acceptable reasons in the two countries, then compare your lists with another person's list.

Apologising

Australians are always apologising; they apologise to everyone, even their family and close friends and for such small things! To me, it feels distant and unfriendly. I don't think you should have to be so polite to friends.

The person who said this had been in Australia for several years and, in spite of extensive contact with Australians, still felt that Australian friendships were basically formal and distant. In pointing to apologies, she was reacting not only to differences between Chinese and Australians in when to apologise but also in who apologises to whom.

Firstly, apologies are very rare in interactions with family and friends. It would not be normal, for example, to apologise for arriving late at a friend's place (though a reason would normally be given) or for telephoning late in the evening. Parents would virtually never apologise to their children nor would husbands and wives apologise to each other.

At the same time, in the wider social context, apologies are less frequent than they are in Australia. It is not usual to apologise after accidentally bumping into someone on the street, when coming in late to class or when asking for information.

However, when differences in status and age are pronounced, apologies are necessary. In such cases, the apology is often conveyed through body language as much as, or even instead of, verbally. A smile, raising the right hand palm outward to shoulder level or lowering the head and bowing slightly forward all constitute socially recognised, and acceptable ways of apologising. Silence also constitutes a powerful apology and is used, together with the appropriate body language, when the person concerned is being criticised.

The use of silence as an apology often contributes to misunderstandings between western teachers and Chinese students. Chinese students typically look down and maintain silence to show contrition when they are criticised by teachers. Many Australian teachers interpret this as defiance. This can result in an escalating loop of miscommunication, as the Australian teacher becomes more and more angry with the Chinese student's continued silence and refusal to look at the teacher in the face, while the student is unable to comprehend the teacher's increasing anger. In the worst case, the teacher concludes that the Chinese student is a disobedient, lazy troublemaker, while the student decides that the teacher's behaviour can only be interpreted as racism.

Another form of apology is likely to result in misunderstanding when it is used with Australians. A Chinese teacher describes her experience in the following way:

My mobile phone rang unexpectedly while I was in a meeting. I felt so ashamed that I ran out quickly while everybody laughed. A few days later another teacher asked me why all her Chinese students kept sticking their tongues out at her: she felt this was very rude. I explained to her that it was only a sheepish expression that could be interpreted as 'I'm sorry' or 'That was a near escape'. On hearing this, the teacher laughed and told me that I had looked very funny with my tongue sticking out when I went back to the room. I didn't even realise that I had made that face!

When do people apologise in English?

List as many situations as possible where an apology is required.

Present this list to your Chinese students. Do they apologise in the same situations?

How is the strength of an apology increased in English?

What determines the strength of the apology used?

Classroom Tasks

■ TASK 1 ■

Kate Hegarty and Han Zhi Jun were good friends. They did a lot of things together and got on well. Recently, though, Kate had been getting more and more dissatisfied with Han. Han would ring up at ten or eleven o'clock at night just to talk, and when they made an arrangement to meet she was often late. Then one evening Kate had a dinner party to which Han Zhi Jun was invited. She didn't come. Instead, at about ten o'clock she rang up to say that she'd had some business to attend to. Kate felt very upset and began to wonder if Han was really a friend or just using her to practise English.

Imagine you are a friend of both Kate and Han. What would you say to each of them to help them save their friendship?

■ TASK 2 ■

Look at the situations listed below. Which of these situations would require an apology in China? Which would require one in Australia?

Grade each situation on a scale from 1–4:

1 = no apology necessary   **2** = weak apology necessary

3 = moderate apology necessary   **4** = strong apology necessary

Situation	Apology required China				Apology required Australia			
	1	2	3	4	1	2	3	4
You can't finish a report before your boss's deadline.								
You arrive ten minutes late for work.								
You telephone a friend after ten o'clock at night.								

Situation	Apology required China				Apology required Australia			
	1	2	3	4	1	2	3	4
You planned to see a film with a friend, but at the last minute something comes up and you can't go.								
You lose a friend's book.								
A shop assistant gives you the wrong change.								
You have to leave class early.								
You break a beautiful glass belonging to your friend.								
You punish your son for doing something wrong, but then you find out that he didn't do it.								
You want to borrow a library book but you have left your card at home.								

■ TASK 3 ■

When you have finished Task 2, choose one of the situations. With a partner, write a dialogue to fit the situation. Your teacher will check the appropriateness of what you say.

■ TASK 4 ■

How would you change your apology in the following circumstances?

With a partner, act out each of these situations, showing the differences.

a. At a friend's house you spill some coffee on the floor. It's easy to clean up.

b. At a friend's house you spill some coffee on their new carpet.

c. At work you knock over your supervisor's cup of coffee. Luckily, it is almost empty and no damage is done.

d. At work you knock over your supervisor's cup of coffee. The coffee spills over many of the papers on his desk.

Offering, declining and accepting

Every Chinese who has had any contact with English speakers has the same story to tell about offering and declining. They are invited to an English speaker's home. The hostess asks them if they'd like a drink and they politely decline. So the hostess sits down and starts talking to them while they get thirstier and thirstier.

The story is common, because the situation does happen frequently. In the equivalent situation in China, nothing would actually be offered at all. Instead, the hostess would automatically give the guest something to drink, usually either tea or a soft drink, and put out some snacks – sweets, sunflower seeds and fruit are common. If something were offered, it would be politely declined, but this would be disregarded.

This situation also extends to eating together. In any semi-formal or formal situation (that is, any situation not involving close friends or family) the host or hostess (who is responsible for ordering if in a restaurant) will simply place some food in the guest's bowl. At the same time, they will urge the guest to eat more.

If a gift or gifts are exchanged, the recipient often initially declines but is prevailed upon to accept. However, once having accepted, which is normally done non-verbally, the gift is put aside and not opened until the guests have left. To open a gift immediately can be taken to imply the gift is more important than the giver.

The situation in service encounters is rather different, as people flying with China Airlines have found. The direct translation of one of the standard offers in service transactions comes out as 'Do you want it or not?', which can have a rather unnerving effect on an English speaker at 25 000 feet. If offers are indirect in social situations, they tend to be correspondingly direct in the public domain of service encounters.

Another difference which has resulted in problems relates to the offering of food. A flight attendant on Qantas will typically offer passengers a choice of, say, beef, chicken or fish. The equivalent on a Chinese airline is rice or noodles. This is because a Chinese meal is taken to consist of a staple (rice or noodles) and accompaniments, while English speaking people regard a meal as consisting of a main course (usually meat or fish) accompanied by a staple.

> With specific reference to the functions of offering, accepting and declining, what aspects of a western dinner party might be unfamiliar to a Chinese student?
>
> How might you include some of these problem areas in your teaching?

Classroom Tasks

■ TASK 1 ■

You are writing a handbook to introduce aspects of Australian social life to Chinese students who are preparing to study in Australia.

Write a paragraph on how Australians offer, accept and decline refreshments when their friends visit them. Remember to give examples of what they actually say.

Thanking

Australians are always saying thank you – thank you for this, thank you for that, all sorts of small things. I never remember to say it because really it doesn't mean anything.

This student was voicing a common feeling. It seems to many Chinese that Australians thank people like shop assistants and bank clerks who are only doing their jobs. They thank their friends, who shouldn't need thanking if they are friends and they even thank their family members, just as if they were strangers. And they thank people for such small things, so when there really is something that they want to say 'thank you' for, the thanks is devalued. It no longer has any meaning.

It's obvious from this that the Chinese use of 'thank you' differs radically from the Australian use of the same word. In general, Chinese don't thank for actions that are performed in the course of work. They would also seldom thank their friends, especially for the small things that friends do for each other. Thanking friends can make the relationship feel formal or distant. The excessive use of 'thank you' also tends to sound obsequious. Chinese, therefore, frequently do not thank sufficiently in English and may inadvertently give offence.

Classroom Tasks

■ TASK 1 ■

'It costs nothing to say thanks and it makes things so much nicer. I just don't understand why people don't say it.'

What do you think of this attitude?

■ TASK 2 ■

What differences have you noticed between the way Australians use 'thank you' and the Chinese use *xie xie*?

What advice would you give to a Chinese friend intending to come to Australia regarding the use of 'thank you'?

Requesting assistance

The problem with requesting assistance lies not so much in the actual form of the request (though there is a problem here, related to translation) as in perceptions regarding to whom requests should be directed, and what constitutes an appropriate response to a request.

To deal with the lesser problem first, many Chinese students use as their major request form 'Can you help me?', which is a direct translation from the Chinese. Unfortunately, in Chinese it functions as a common but forceful request for assistance, while in English the nearest analogue is restricted to service encounters.

Perceptions regarding who to approach for assistance are a greater problem. In general it is felt that the more senior a person, the more useful it is to approach them with a request. People will therefore often attempt to circumvent the chain of command in a way that may be interpreted by Australians as going behind the back of the person in question.

A Chinese worker or student may feel that it is a waste of time to go through her immediate superior if that person does not have the power to grant the request. She may therefore directly approach the person who does have that power, feeling that direct lobbying is more likely to be successful than an approach mediated through a third party.

Alternatively, if the initial request is refused, the person making the request may then attempt to go over the head of her immediate supervisor in an effort to get the decision reversed. In both cases, the person making the request is likely to antagonise the people in charge.

A further complication arises when we examine the attitude of the worker or student to his immediate superior. He is likely to feel that the superior has a duty to represent his opinions to those in authority. In other words, people in the intermediate levels of a hierarchy may be expected to champion, or at least to effectively represent, the opinions of those below. The refusal of a request for assistance may therefore be interpreted as the result of ineffective representation on the part of those occupying intermediate positions. This may be an added incentive for a direct approach to the top. It may also result in resentment against people in intermediate positions, who may be felt to be intentionally failing to fulfil their responsibilities.

Classroom Tasks

■ TASK 1 ■

Gao Yang was working in an Australian company. Because of some urgent personal business he was forced to apply for a week's leave. Unfortunately, this occurred at the busiest time of the year for the company and the request was refused. When his supervisor told him that his request had been refused, Gao Yang said nothing, but the next day went to see the director of the company in person. His request was again refused and the director was clearly very displeased to see him. Gao Yang's supervisor was also obviously displeased.

Why were Gao Yang's supervisor and the director of the company displeased with him?

What advice would you give him to prevent the situation arising again?

■ TASK 2 ■

Many of the students at the Newcross Language Centre wanted to study in evening courses. However, the head of the centre, while recognising that the students really needed evening classes, claimed that it was impossible to grant their requests because all the evening classes were full. The students knew that there were several unoccupied classrooms in the evenings where classes could be held. They therefore asked the head to explain their position to the regional director so that he would authorise more evening classes. However nothing happened. The students became very unhappy and felt betrayed by the head, who had seemed to agree with their requests.

Were the students justified in feeling betrayed?

Asking for information

Asking for information in a service encounter tends to be more direct in Chinese than it is in English, because it involves people doing their jobs. As such, they do not need to be thanked, nor are softened forms used, though it is usual to use the equivalent of 'please'. Students may have a tendency to use very direct forms when speaking English rather than the softened forms which are more generally used by Australians, even when the softened forms are within their linguistic competence.

CHAPTER SEVEN

ATTITUDES AND VALUES

In this chapter, we are mainly concerned with some of the ideas that influence people's thinking. We will focus on concepts that play a key role in how people interpret the world, concepts which are significantly different from the ideas that the average Australian uses to order and comprehend the world. These concepts are of importance in communication because they are a major influence on both the behaviour of the individual and the interpretation of others' behaviour. Major differences in such key ideas as the concept of face or the way that social relationships are organised may result in inappropriate behaviour or the inappropriate attribution of meaning to others' behaviour.

In examining these concepts, the aim is not to judge or decide that one is somehow better than the other. Rather, the aim is to help establish a mutual understanding, to allow teachers, businesspeople and others some insight into why the Chinese people with whom they are interacting are reacting as they are, and to likewise help Chinese people in Australia interpret the behaviour not only of their teachers but also of the Australians with whom they interact.

Face

When talking to Australians about their experiences in China or with Chinese people, face is often one of the first issues that comes up. Australians tend to be very aware that it is important not to cause Chinese people to lose face. They will often go on to remark that they themselves don't care whether they lose face or not, as they don't feel that they have any face to lose. Face then is seen as in some way not quite rational, an affectation that all would be better without, but one that has to be accommodated.

Before examining the usefulness of this perception, it is worth establishing what exactly is meant by face.[1] Sociologists and sociolinguists usually define face as the public image that each participant in an interaction wants to project about him or herself. It also refers to the public image that each participant in an interaction grants the other. Looked at in this way, face is partly negotiated between the participants in an interaction and partly established by situational factors such as relative age, position, gender and so on.

This definition is useful, but it needs to be taken further by considering two different aspects of any interaction. The first is the need to be usefully involved and to be seen to be involved in an interaction. This aspect of an interaction stresses the need to be seen as an effective and contributing member of society.

The second concerns the need to maintain personal independence and to respect the personal independence of others. We can say, then, that we need to recognise two different ways of looking at face: involvement face and independence face. Chinese and Australians (and indeed all English speaking cultures) recognise both aspects of face, but value them differently, with Chinese emphasising involvement face and Australians stressing independence face. In other words, a Chinese person is more likely to react strongly to a threat to his or her involvement face, while an Australian is more likely to react to a threat to his or her independence face.

The following example illustrates how this difference works out in practice. One late Sunday afternoon just as I was leaving home to attend a family gathering, the phone rang. It was a Chinese acquaintance inviting me to dinner that very evening and asking what time she should pick me up! At the time I felt annoyed at her lack of consideration in inviting me so late, and told her that I could not possibly come as I had already made other plans. She was clearly surprised and unhappy at my response. As we each replaced our respective phones, both of us felt hurt and even to some extent insulted. It was only later, reflecting on the incident, that I realised that my annoyance stemmed from feeling that my freedom of action had been infringed, that I had been denied choice and that my participation had been taken for granted. In short, my independence face had been infringed.

My Chinese acquaintance, on the other hand, felt hurt because I had inadvertently infringed her involvement face in several ways. Firstly, I had refused without fully explaining why I could not accept. Had I explained carefully that I was committed to attending a family gathering, I would have given her a graceful way out. Offering a graceful retreat was doubly important because my friend would have known that she was at fault in inviting me at such late notice. To put this another way, she knew that she should have invited me earlier, and she knew that I knew. An Australian in this situation would apologise for the late notice, but in the Chinese context, apologies between friends are inappropriate. As was pointed out in Chapter 6, page 97, they are regarded as overpolite, and in this situation would have signalled a significant cooling of our relationship. It was therefore incumbent on me to show my compassion and understanding of her predicament by allowing her a way out. This I did not do. For her, it must have felt like a slap in the face (no pun intended!).

The situation was exacerbated by the form of the invitation, which I experienced as a demand. For my friend, however, its forceful phrasing was intended to indicate that the invitation was genuine, as opposed to a general expression of good will of the 'Let's have coffee sometime' variety. So what I experienced as disregard for my feelings and plans was meant by her as an expression of her regard for me. Unfortunately, it took some time before the offence inadvertently given by both sides was overcome.

The importance of different conceptions of face most obviously arises in the context of business, and Chapter 8 will examine more fully the ways in which these two aspects of face influence business relationships.

We started this discussion of face by pointing out that many Australians tend to see face as something uniquely Chinese, and in a sense illegitimate, because it tends to get in the way of the efficient conduct of relationships. There is often the feeling that if Chinese just dropped their worry about how others see them, admitted mistakes when they were made, accepted public criticism and so on, then everything would be easy and all would be better off. The Chinese themselves, it is often felt, would be grateful for such relief. These same Australians might try asking themselves how they would feel if their freedom of action was curtailed and their decisions constantly monitored or countermanded: in other words, how they react to infringements of their independence face. This exercise gives some insight into how many Chinese feel about threats to their involvement face.

Think about your own situation.

a. What type of actions at work or in the classroom make you feel threatened and uncomfortable?

b. To what extent do you think such actions might be classified as threats to your involvement face or threats to your independence face?

c. If you are a teacher, how might your actions infringe the involvement face of your students?

Personal involvement: The importance of *guanxi*

Guanxi (*guanshi*) is one of the keys to life in China. It is usually translated as 'relation' or 'relationship', but the translation does not do justice to the full meaning of the word.[2]

Guanxi refers to the development and use of the network of mutual obligations that bind people together. These include relationships founded on family ties, neighbourly ties and ties springing from common geographic origins, ties of shared experience and ties of shared interest. It involves the use of such personal ties to circumvent bureaucratic procedures, obtain access to scarce resources and ensure preferential treatment. Some Australians see *guanxi* as synonymous with corruption, but to interpret it in this way is to misunderstand both the term itself and the context in which it occurs.

In order to fully understand the nature and importance of *guanxi*, we need to first explore another concept, *renqing* (*renching*), which can be translated as 'human feelings'. *Renqing* is what characterises relationships: it is the natural feeling of affection and interdependence that exists between people. More, it is the glue which keeps society together. A person who lacks *renqing* lacks an essential component of what it means to be human.

Crucially, *renqing* involves the recognition of ties of mutual obligation between individuals, so it is a concrete rather than an abstract relationship: it is embodied in the ways that people act towards each other. This means that it also involves appropriate behaviour, paying respect to and looking after older members of the family, assisting younger people, giving a gift in thanks for a favour, and so on. Relationships characterised by *renqing* cannot be limited to a single interaction, they are ongoing, with each interaction contributing to the development of a web of social relationships characterised by warmth, trust and mutuality.

The *guanxi* relationship is not the same as the *renqing* relationship, but it draws on the concepts embodied in that relationship and can be seen in many ways as the instrumentalisation of *renqing*. It involves a network of personal ties characterised by mutual obligation which can, as outlined above, be used to obtain the necessities of everyday life: finding a job, getting a permit, gaining admission to a particular school or university. In the business sphere, *guanxi* ties facilitate a whole range of activities and necessities, from ensuring a reliable electricity supply to negotiating the amount of tax a company needs to pay. The important thing about *guanxi* is that, like *renqing*, it involves mutual obligation, and that it is a relationship that exists between individuals, even when those individuals are acting on behalf of a company or an institution.

Some examples of the use of *guanxi* in the private sphere will illustrate how the system works; examples of the importance of *guanxi* in the business sphere are given in Chapter 8, page 134. University entrance is highly competitive in China, and there are always more well-qualified applicants than there are places available. I remember visiting a friend of mine just after the results of the university entrance examinations had been announced. My friend's son had done well, but she wanted to ensure that he was accepted into the course of his choice at the university of his choice. It happened that an old acquaintance was working in the faculty in question. In fact, the two of them had been in the countryside together during the Cultural Revolution. My friend was therefore preparing to go and see him, and was taking some fresh fish as a gift. She was sure that, once reminded of their relationship, her son would have no problem in being accepted, and the fish would be seen as an expression of thanks, but not necessarily as a complete repayment of the debt. She acknowledged that by calling on this old relationship she was incurring an obligation, and that she would be expected to reciprocate if necessary in future.

In another case, a friend's daughter had just graduated from university and was having difficulty finding a job. Her father remembered that he had gone to school with a man who had gone on to study abroad and who had, on his return, founded a small private company. He contacted this person, who was unable himself to employ the daughter, but who was able to give her an introduction to another company which did offer her a job. In this case, the father felt himself indebted to his friend, while his friend was indebted to the owner of the company which finally provided the job. In other words, the *guanxi* relationship is dyadic: it exists between pairs of people. These pairs can form a chain, but obligation is only incurred between two people who are in contact, no matter how long the chain of which they are part is.

If *guanxi* draws on the moral universe of *renqing* in one way, in another way it can shade into corruption. Officially, in fact, *guanxi* is often regarded as corruption because the most effective and useful *guanxi* networks involve people in positions of power who are able to use this power to grant favours. One of the ways that corruption differs from *guanxi* is that corruption does not usually involve the creation of reciprocal ties of obligation: it is a straight-out payment in exchange for a favour. For example, if a person pays an under-the-counter fee for a particular service, say to obtain an official stamp on a document, this is corruption. However, if the person giving the stamp has a personal relationship with the person requesting the stamp, and acknowledges the interaction as part of an ongoing web of mutual obligation, then this is usually regarded as *guanxi*, even if a gift changes hands. If, however, the transactions involved are large enough, then even the existence of mutuality will not necessarily avoid a *guanxi* relationship being considered as corruption. This indicates another aspect of *guanxi*: the way in which it is perceived by the public at large.

When party members, officials and other such people use their positions in order to access scarce resources themselves or to regulate the access of others, it causes a great deal of public anger. Indeed, it is this kind of behaviour that is the chief cause of dissatisfaction with Party rule, and was one of the most important underlying causes of the events leading up to the Tiananmen massacre in 1989. However, if a person refuses to assist a friend or neighbour to find a job, or a relation to get a difficult-to-obtain ticket to a popular concert, then that person may well be regarded as lacking in feeling. The public perception of *guanxi* is therefore complex and judgments around it need to be carefully considered and nuanced.

For Australians, understanding *guanxi* relationships is particularly important in relation to doing business, and this is discussed in greater detail in Chapter 8, page 134.

Hierarchy

Traditional Chinese ethics held it as self-evident that society was hierarchical. Of the five relationships that together were considered to form the foundations of civilised society – those between ruler and subject, father and son, husband and wife, elder brother and younger brother and between friends – the first four were hierarchical relationships, with the junior (or female) owing respect and obedience to the senior (or male). In return, the senior was expected to exercise benevolence, fairness and justice in guiding those below him.

The idea that all men and women were equal was held to be obviously false; some people were naturally more intelligent, more capable than others. Educated people were obviously better fitted to lead than uneducated people. More seriously it was a fundamental violation of morality and the natural order of the world. If sons did not respect their fathers, and subjects their ruler, then the whole social fabric, a social fabric built on the recognition of mutual obligation and the importance of social harmony, was under threat.

In today's China, hierarchic social relationships continue to dominate and to be valued in ways which many Australians, with their more egalitarian beliefs, find difficult to understand. It is not uncommon for Australians to approach relations with Chinese people with the unstated assumption that things will move more swiftly if hierarchical distinctions are minimised, and in the belief that this minimisation will be welcomed by all concerned. This attitude can result in serious miscommunication, as many Chinese are likely to interpret attempts at equality as lack of respect, and may actively resist moves to downplay distinctions. This is especially important in the business sphere and is discussed in greater detail in Chapter 8.

One of the most important ways in which the hierarchic organisation of social life is displayed is in respect for age and authority. This is strongly reflected in language. Older people and superiors are often addressed as *nin*, the more respectful of the two words that translate into the English 'you'. Language addressed to them is usually less direct than language addressed to contemporaries or equals. Orders, for example, are avoided. Requests are phrased indirectly and prefaced with statements of regret for causing trouble. Opinions, if expressed, are tentative, apologies strongly worded. The relative difference in age and status between two people talking tends therefore to be more strongly marked in Chinese than it is in English. This may result in Chinese learners appearing over-respectful when speaking to older Australians or those in higher positions.

At the same time, when addressing friends, younger people or those in subordinate positions, the language used tends to be more direct than would be the case in English. Commands are widely used and differences of opinion forcefully voiced. Translated into English, such language may appear brusque to the point of rudeness.

Chinese coming to Australia may be puzzled by Australians' overt emphasis on equality. Many, especially the elderly or those who occupied senior positions in China, may resent being deprived of what they feel is due respect. Some may go further and ascribe this neglect as racism. Most people are also likely to feel uncomfortable when they are discouraged from paying respect where they feel it is necessary. Young adults, for example, often find it difficult to address older Australians by their first names and most Chinese university students never adjust to calling their lecturers by first name.

Lack of familiarity with English ways of showing respect may cause people to remain silent rather than risk offence through lack of respect. Teachers need to remember that learners are likely to use relative age and status as a primary determinant of the level of politeness to be used, and this may result in socially inappropriate speech.

Australian attitudes to the aged are likely to be regarded as shocking, even fundamentally immoral. It is widely believed that Australians do not acknowledge any responsibility to their parents and are guilty of abuse and neglect in their dealing with the elderly. On the other hand, the casual and often contemptuous attitude of Australians towards political leaders tends to provoke a kind of scandalised delight.

The concept of the individual

For most Australians, individualism is an unquestioned positive value. Individual self-fulfilment and the maximal realisation of individual potential are legitimate and often-expressed aims in life. The various state education systems have as one of their primary aims the fostering of a sense of individualism and of the means of realising that individualism. The individual is held to have legitimate interests and rights that are separate from, and may even be antagonistic to, the interests of the family, the community or the state. In fact, individual interests tend to be considered as primary, and individuals are considered justified in protecting their interests from intrusion in the name of other institutions and interests.

This view contrasts sharply with the view of most Chinese, a view grounded in traditional Confucian philosophy. According to this view, the individual exists in and through society. Alone, in isolation, he or she has no meaningful existence. Private interests are vested in the group, that is, in the family or in the community and not in the individual. The individual per se therefore has few legitimate private interests separate from those of the group. Any attempt to set up individual interests in opposition to those of society merely demonstrates a selfish refusal to recognise the necessity of social relationships and a reluctance to carry out social responsibilities. True self-fulfilment for the individual lies in fulfilling social responsibilities to the greatest extent possible.

As individual interests are subsumed in group interests, so the establishment and maintenance of social harmony is valued over the exercise of individual rights. In fact, the establishment of harmonious social relations is seen as an absolute necessity, without which any development is impossible.

The contrast between the Australian and the Chinese moral system, then, can be understood as a contrast between a rights-based system and a duties-based system. The duties of a Chinese to his or her family, to society and the country, tend to outweigh rights as an individual.

The western concept of individualism, which opposes social and individual interests, appears to many Chinese as extremely selfish, and many of the perceived evils of Australian society are blamed on this selfish insistence on the priority of the self. The high divorce rate, for example, is often attributed to Australians' willingness to put individual benefit before that of the family, children and society. Old people are also seen as victims of individualism, their children abandoning them because they interfere in their pursuit of self-interest.

The supremacy of social over individual interests and the equation of individual interests with selfishness have a major effect on other key social concepts, notably those relating to the powers and responsibilities of government and the social basis of law. These will be examined in the following section.

The role of government

Traditional Chinese theories of government all stress the hierarchic nature of society and draw parallels between the authority structure of the family and the authority structure of the state. Thus a ruler is to his subjects as the father is to his children, a husband to his wife or an elder brother to a younger brother. In all these relationships the latter is subordinate to the former, the superior embodying and acting in accordance with the interests of the group, whether that group be the family, the community or the nation.

The duty of the ruler is to provide a stable and peaceful environment in which groups such as the family can productively exist and to enable the community as a whole to develop. Such an environment is best provided by a ruler who complies with the moral rules of society, being filial, loyal and compassionate. Acting in this way, the ruler inspires others to do the same and the beneficial effects are felt throughout society. If the ruler fails to live up to the accepted moral code, then it is the duty of his advisers to criticise him and to remind him of the expected standards of behaviour.

Since 1949 the Communist Party has occupied the role of ruler, regarding itself as embodying the interests of the working class and beyond that the interests of most sections of the community. Specifically excluded, however were groups such as 'feudal landlords' and 'bureaucratic capitalists' over whom the party exercised 'people's dictatorship'. The rapid development of the private sector of the economy since the 1980s has resulted in a major change in this respect, with Party membership being opened to leading businesspeople in 2001. The Party is thus in a position to claim that it represents the interests of the vast majority of the population, including the 'advanced productive forces' and the 'advanced cultural forces'.

This does not mean, however, that opposition is tolerated or regarded in any way as legitimate. Those who are categorised as actively opposing the Party are also deemed to be opposing the state and as such are not considered to have legitimate interests. The state, in fact, is not only justified in not representing the interests of such people, but is also justified in restricting or suspending their rights for the good of the wider society. Groups in this category include political dissidents, unregulated religious groups such as Falungong (a group which draws on Buddhist and Daoist beliefs and practises meditation and Tai Chi), worker activists campaigning for workers' rights and their overseas supporters and so on.

The interests of the Party, then, are identified with the interests of the state. In spite of attempts in the past 20 years to distinguish the roles of state, Party and government in national life, the equation state = government = Party is still valid. As such it is the state/government/Party's duty to ensure the development of the country and the welfare of each section of the community. With regard to the former, the Party is therefore responsible for the fair and equitable distribution and efficient management of the resources of the state, and for the efficient management of government so that development is maximised.

At the same time, the welfare of each section of the community must be ensured with the guarantee of the basic necessities of life. Several guarantees are in fact written into the constitution, including the right to food, clothing, fuel, schooling and work. Not all these guarantees in fact apply, all being dependent on the capacity of the state to grant them. All can be restricted if it is in society's interest to do so. In general it is also expected that the government will ensure a stable social environment; that is, that prices will not rise, that the crime rate will be low and that government officials will not use their positions to enrich themselves.

Failure to provide either the constitutionally guaranteed necessities or those that are generally socially accepted as being the government's responsibility may result in the widespread questioning of the Party/government's claim to represent community and national interests and thus their right to continue in power.

A key difference between Chinese and Australian attitudes to government lies in the definition of democracy. In the western tradition accepted in Australia, the primary meaning of democracy is that those who govern are selected by the adult population of a state through the ballot box. The government can and should be changed at regular intervals without threatening the interests of the state. This ability to change governments through election constitutes a major bulwark against the abuse of power and is necessary to ensure that individual rights are maintained against the encroaching power of the state. Careful distinctions are made between the state, the government and political parties, with the right to rule being a legitimate object of political struggle.

That the Chinese concept of democracy is quite different is obvious from the demands raised in the so-called Democracy Movement which culminated in 1989. During this movement, the demand for popular elections was never raised, though calls for 'democracy' were constant. What was being demanded was not that power holders be elected but that they carry out their responsibilities by ending inflation, wiping out corruption and preventing the misuse of power for personal ends.

Dialogue with the government was demanded, rather than the ability to choose the government.

This view of democracy is implicit in both the traditional and the Marxist views of government described above. It accepts that the interests of society can be embodied in a single entity, in this case the Party, and that there is no real conflict between individual interests and the broader interests of community. It does, however, demand that the Party be judged by its performance. Should the Party fail to carry out its duties as government, the community has a moral duty to remind it of its responsibilities. A government that refuses to listen to such protests is likely to lose its right to govern.

Internal party documents relating to the transfer of power to the new generation of leaders who took over in 2002 reveal that the Party leadership does in fact regard the major threat to its legitimacy not as political dissent but as popular dissatisfaction with high levels of corruption within the Party and more broadly within society at large. Li Ruihuan, Chairman of the Standing Committee of the National People's Congress and occupying the second most important place in the hierarchy of leadership, commented as follows:

> To be sure, people's living standards today are greatly improved over what they were in the 1950s and 1960s or even the 1970s. In some places they have even reached, or gotten close to, the level of mid-level developing countries in Asia or in the world. But take notice: Which section of the people are those [who are better off?] [They are Party members who have benefited from power to gain wealth.] This is why feelings of anger, cursing, resistance, and oppositional emotions have risen to an all-time high. To be sure, people enjoy freedoms under the constitution that are the broadest freedoms in our history. But take notice: Which group of people enjoy freedoms and rights that go beyond those guaranteed in the constitution? This is why people's criticism, denunciation, resistance, and cries of opposition to the Party and to leading cadres have come to the boiling point.
>
> Nathan and Gilley 2002: 193

Current discussions on political reform focus on two different approaches. The first involves reform of the Party through the strengthening of internal Party mechanisms, specifically through improved selection, evaluation and training of Party members. Increased use of internal Party elections is seen as part of this strategy as such elections give a measure of power to the Party rank and file and encourage the leadership to take their views into consideration.

The second approach involves increasing the power of ordinary people to supervise the work of Party and government through media oversight and the greater use of elections. Reformers supporting these measures aim to reduce controls on the media, allowing greater scrutiny of Party and government actions. They also advocate expanding elections from the village level to township and later county, city and provincial levels. Such elections would, however, be open to individuals, but not to organised political parties.

Both approaches to political reform are based on improving accountability and efficiency in the exercise of power, rather than on changing the holders of state power.

There are, of course, a number of people who advocate a much more thorough process of reform and the introduction of a multiparty democracy, but they are at present a minority.

The general and expected attitude towards government leaders is one of respect. Most people in normal circumstances feel that government policies are likely to be based on reason, even if this is not immediately apparent to the person on the street. Many, particularly but certainly not only, in the countryside tend to feel that government and government policies are none of their business. It is only when the government manifestly fails to provide what it should provide that most take an interest in politics.

When Chinese come to Australia from China, they may find many aspects of the political system puzzling. Some may believe that the government has the moral responsibility to provide them with employment. This belief is reinforced by the wide range of welfare benefits available in Australia but not in China. If the government is prepared to offer such secondary benefits, then surely it must also guarantee the primary ones!

Politically, the concept of an independent, legal opposition, the open criticism and mockery of government figures and the generally negative attitude of Australians towards their government and towards politicians of all complexions may cause confusion. People may also be reluctant to discuss politics, particularly Chinese politics, with people they do not know.

More importantly, many Chinese may be reluctant to have any contact with the political system at all. They may fear that any attempt to approach or to use the political system will only result in inviting unnecessary attention from the authorities. Such attention is seen as inevitably resulting in trouble, as the political system and the authorities which embody it are not regarded as being open or responsive to the individual or to individual pressure.

They may also be intensely suspicious of government departments and be extremely reluctant to divulge personal information to authorised government bodies. Guarantees of confidentiality are widely disbelieved.

The concept of law

A fundamental difference in concept divides Chinese and Australian law. Most western legal systems, including that of Australia, are based on the concept of natural law. Natural law is inherent in nature and therefore in humankind; it exists and has a binding ethical force independent of the interests of particular communities, groups or individuals.

In contrast, the Chinese historically regard law as being made by people to serve social (that is, group or collective) purposes. Law expresses ethically binding principles, but they are principles enunciated by humankind, and accepted by humankind, in order to enhance the general good of society. In practice, this means that law tends to be particularistic and situational, serving particular groups in particular situations at particular times.

In modern China, law continues to be seen as serving the interests of particular social groups. Thus there is bourgeois law, which expresses the interests of the ruling class in capitalist societies, and there is socialist law, expressing the interests of the working class. No pretence is made of an impartial law; law is frankly acknowledged as partisan. Human rights, for example, are regarded as being bestowed on the population by the government. They are therefore open to restriction on the grounds of social interest and do not automatically apply to all people. The right to free speech or freedom of religion, for example, is subordinate to the need to maintain social stability and more recently investor confidence.

A further important difference between Australian and Chinese law relates to precedent. Australian common law relates to British common law and is based on precedent rather than on a body of what might be called legislative law. Precedent is not regarded as having legal validity in China, a position that again results from the conception of law as serving sectional interests. According to this view, all pre-1949 law represents the interests of the bourgeoisie and as such is inappropriate for a socialist state.

Regarding law as a valid expression of social interests means that the authority to make law lies not only with the organs of state or government but also with the Communist Party, representing as it claims the interests of the vast majority of the population. In formal terms, the Party does not in fact have the legal power to enact laws, but regional party leaders do have the power to issue binding regulations. The practical effect of this has been to give high ranking party functionaries quasi-legal powers. This system has frequently resulted in the substitution of individual fiat for the rule of law, particularly, but certainly not only, during times of turmoil such as the Cultural Revolution.

In the past 20 years major efforts have been made to vest lawmaking powers in organs of state and to reduce the role of the Party, thereby standardising the law and abolishing the arbitrary and individual power of local bodies. Particularism, however, remains strong, in that laws passed by the central government are often interpreted by local and provincial-level authorities in ways that are seen as suiting local conditions. A common complaint from foreign businesspeople is that different interpretations of the same law are given in different provinces, necessitating a regional rather than a national approach to business.

As was historically the case, the major task of the modern body of law is to ensure social stability. It is therefore primarily a body of criminal law. Recently, however, a great deal of effort has gone into developing a body of commercial law, now seen as necessary in order to facilitate both domestic economic development and foreign investment.

Another interesting development is the introduction of laws allowing citizens to sue individuals, companies and government agencies, laws which have resulted in many thousands of suits. Obviously such suits are costly and usually beyond the reach of the poorer members of the community, although it is precisely such people who are most in need of protection against oppressive and greedy local authorities. In recognition of this fact, there have been moves towards establishing a legal aid program, and such a program was established in 1999 in Guangdong. This program has funded a large number of cases often on behalf of migrant workers, who constitute the most vulnerable section of the population. Legal aid is not, however, available to people charged with criminal offences. Rather, it constitutes another weapon in the fight to make state institutions accountable and responsive to the public, and is thus an aspect of the political reform process.

If the law itself is not seen as independent, neither is its administration. Chinese courts are openly recognised as instruments of particular social interests. They do not constitute impartial arenas where individuals defend their individual interests. They are presided over by judges who are public servants and usually party members, who see their task as ensuring social stability and enforcing party/government/class interests. The right of defence is recognised but is in fact limited to the right to plead in mitigation. Lawyers who defend their clients too vigorously run the risk of being accused together with their clients.

Great emphasis is placed on the accused's confession of guilt, those who refuse to confess are regarded as unrepentant rather than not guilty and so given heavier punishment. Obviously there is no presumption of innocence, rather the reverse. Once a person is arrested, they are widely regarded as guilty and proving otherwise is extremely difficult.

The right of appeal is recognised but in practice tends to be a formality. Cases are often dealt with extremely quickly, especially at times when the government deems it expedient to encourage social stability. At such times, many normally accepted legal procedures are suspended and it is not unknown for a person to be arrested, tried and convicted, to appeal, lose and be shot within a week.

In general, punishments are severe. The death penalty is extensively used and its use raises little or no opposition. It is widely felt that criminals, in particular those guilty of serious crimes such as murder, rape and armed robbery, have by their actions so violated social norms that their deaths are in the community interest. Since 1997, the 'strike hard' campaign has aimed to stamp out all threats to social order, and resulted in 60 000 people being put to death in the period from 1998 to 2001.[3]

Apart from the death penalty, there are two major forms of imprisonment. 'Labour re-education' allows a person to be sentenced to up to four years of hard labour on a police order alone and without appearing in court. This form of detention is aimed at 'hooligans' and people considered to have 'anti-socialist views'. 'Labour reform' is more serious. A person so sentenced is convicted in court and sentences tend to be very long by Australian standards. People in this category range from common criminals to those whose crime is opposing the government, usually referred to as jeopardising the security of the country.

In settling in Australia, Chinese are likely to find many aspects of our legal system confusing at best, and at worst incomprehensible. Firstly, many are likely to be extremely distrustful of the police, who may be feared as the unpredictable wielders of arbitrary power. People are extremely unlikely to voluntarily cooperate with the police, believing that to invite unnecessary attention is likely to result in problems.

In the event of being arrested, some may immediately plead guilty, regardless of the truth of the plea, in the belief that it is impossible to escape punishment and that a guilty plea will reduce the likely sentence. Many may be unaware of their right to legal representation or that such representation may in fact be useful.

As China has little consumer law, many will be ignorant of their rights in this respect. They are also likely to disregard the ability of the courts to settle commercial disputes. In fact, many may not recognise the range of law and its applications in Australia. Many Chinese regard Australian punishments as ridiculously lenient, and this tends to heighten the common perception that Australian society is lawless and dangerous.

The sense of history

It is almost impossible to be Chinese without having an extraordinarily strong awareness of being heir to 5000 years of history. This does not mean that, as has sometimes been alleged, Chinese culture is a culture exclusively concerned with the past. Even less does it mean that, as individuals, people are well informed about the actual events of their history. What it does mean is that the past is seen as offering a guide to the present. It presents an enormous series of precedents which can be consulted in order to decide on a correct path of action. It also means that in seeking explanations of events or circumstances, there is a strong tendency to seek historical explanations. Events, circumstances and happenings are seen as embedded in a historical context that is of primary importance in their interpretation. As a result, problems, including academic problems, tend to be first situated in their historical context. From the Australian point of view, this situating may appear irrelevant.

The past in itself, those 5000 years (or 3000 or 6000, depending on which starting point is chosen) of history, is both a source of pride and national identity, and a burden. As a source of pride it is a vital component of the Chinese sense of national identity. Chinese philosophy and literature, Chinese painting, pottery and calligraphy are rightly seen as among the supreme achievements of human civilisation. They are the products of an empire and a civilisation that dominated the eastern world for 2000 years. This greatness is strongly felt to be the heritage of every Chinese.

At the same time, the past is a burden, an enormous brake on development. This sense of the past is summed up in the word 'feudal'. Formally, 'feudalism' in Chinese Marxist historiography refers to the entire historical period from the founding of the Han Dynasty in 206 BC to the European encroachments in the mid-19th century. In everyday speech, it refers to the complex of institutions and values believed to have characterised the feudal period, including autocracy, bureaucracy, conservatism and distrust of the foreign or the new. The continuation of these attitudes in modern China is seen by many intellectuals as one of the primary causes of China's lack of development. From this point of view, the past is a dead hand that weighs on the back of each succeeding generation, crushing all forms of independent human endeavour.

Different reactions to this dichotomy are illustrated in two important works, one from the late 1980s, the other from the mid-1990s. The first was a six-part television series entitled *Heshang*, 'River Elegy'. The 'river' of the title is the Yellow River, long a symbol of China and of the Chinese. The series identified the inward-looking focus on the past that the writers felt was the essence of the Yellow River symbol as the major cause of China's backwardness. It called for a break with this view, a turning outward to the world and for a flood which would wash away the old and inaugurate a new civilisation.

Heirs of the dragon, everything that the Yellow River has had to give, it has given to our ancestors. They created a civilisation, but the river cannot give birth a second time. We need to create a new civilisation; this time it cannot pour forth from the Yellow River. Like the silt accumulated on the bed of the Yellow River, the old civilisation has left a sediment in the veins of our nation. Only a deluge can purge us of its dregs.

Such a flood is industrial civilisation, and it beckons us.

Heshang Episode 1: 'Searching for Dreams',
quoted in Barmé, G., & Jaivin, L. (1992). *New ghosts, old dreams.*
Times Books, Random House: p 138.

The second, *China can say no*, was a book edited by Zhang Xiaodong and Song Qiang and published in 1996. The book advocates a rejection of 'westernisation', which refers in the main to American influence, and calls for a policy of 'eastern-inspired' development, that is built on Chinese traditions. In a piece for the *New Perspectives Quarterly*, the two editors summed up their ideas as follows:

A generation of Chinese has totally and uncritically absorbed western, particularly American, values. Lately, however, the tide has begun to turn. More and more people in China are looking East instead of West to find a future. Because of the growth of the Chinese economy and the legacy of China's rich cultural traditions, many of us maintain that China should aspire to take its place as a world power instead of lamely emulating western society as, for example, Japan has. ... The sense of loss and resentment at this overwhelming western influence in the Third World is a breeding ground for a growing anti-western post-colonialism. As a consequence, saying no to America will become more and more common in the world, particularly in Asia. ... Examining the state of United States–China relations, we are pessimistic about the future. The younger generation China can't stand America's disingenuous preachiness on human rights (haven't we all seen the video of Rodney King or of the immigrant workers being mercilessly beaten by police in Riverside, California?) or its irresponsible threats on trade sanctions and Taiwan. ... At the end of the 20th century, China has once again become a world power in its own right. It need not play second fiddle to anyone. The next generation coming to power in China is prepared to say no and won't hesitate to do so when it is in our interests.

Zhang Xiaodong & Song Qiang. (1996). 'China Can Say No',
New Perspectives Quarterly, 13(4), p 55.

For thinkers such as Zhang Xiaodong and Song Qiang, the Chinese past offers an alternative and more appropriate basis for national development, but one that will inevitably involve conflict with the United States. The reasons for this will be examined in the next section.

Patriotism, nationalism and attitudes to the West

Patriotism is a highly valued virtue in Chinese culture and one that has had strong official encouragement since the end of the Cultural Revolution. It has since then formed the cornerstone of the government's efforts to rally popular support behind the Party and its modernisation program.

Patriotism rests heavily on three key elements. The first has already been discussed: the sense of pride in China's immense cultural and historic achievements. This is accompanied by a love of the natural beauty of China, of her lakes and rivers and especially of the thousands of areas of scenic beauty that have classical associations.

The second element relates to who exactly is considered Chinese. The answer is given in physical terms – the Chinese are the yellow race: 'yellow-skinned, black-eyed, black-haired' as it is usually expressed.

The third element is the enormous sense of resentment and betrayal that is felt by many Chinese as a result of the past 150 years of history. The period starting with the Opium Wars of the mid-19th century and continuing to 1949 and the declaration of the People's Republic of China is seen as a time of unmitigated national humiliation. During this time China lost position as one of the great powers of the world. China was subjected to invasion first by European powers and then by the Japanese, and came very close to being reduced to a series of colonies. That a considerable part of the blame for this catastrophic period of history is now laid at the door of the then-ruling Manchu (and therefore non-Han) Qing Dynasty, and of the Chiang Kaishek regime which fled to Taiwan at the end of the Civil War in 1949 in no way reduces the sense of shame that underlies some Chinese attitudes to the rest of the world.

The opening to the outside world that has taken place over the last 20 years has allowed people to compare China's development with that of the western world and Japan. This has for some fuelled a feeling of anger which informs the sense of nationalism discussed in the preceding section. Such people feel that China, by virtue of size and population, long history and enormous cultural achievements, should be recognised as a world power, and that if China is not seen as this, it is the result of a deliberate negative campaign. Responsibility for this campaign is usually slated home to the United States. It is here that patriotism merges with nationalism.

The situation is complicated by a perception of international relations which is somewhat different from that prevailing in Australia and other western countries. For most Australians, the international arena is populated by a large number of states which compete with each other. Powers rise and fall in this arena, evidenced, for example, by the collapse of the Soviet Union and the emergence of a single great power in the 1990s. Importantly, no country is seen as occupying a leading role by right. This is not however a concept shared by many Chinese, who take a position that is informed by the hierarchic approach to human relationships outlined above.

With respect to international relations, this position involves the expectation that countries occupy more or less fixed positions in an international hierarchy based on size, population, history and culture as well as control of economic and technological resources. On this basis, China's position as a world power should be respected: the country should be treated as an equal by other world powers, and notably by the United States. This is not seen to be so. The feeling of grievance that this gives rise to has been fed by a number of incidents in the late 1990s and the early years of the 21st century. These include the bombing of the Chinese embassy in Belgrade in 1999, the collision of a United States spy plane with a Chinese fighter and the subsequent death of the Chinese pilot in 2001, ongoing support for Taiwan and the loss of the 2000 Olympics to Australia, which was widely seen as having been engineered by anti-China forces in the United States.

If China itself should occupy a leading role on the world stage, smaller countries, and particularly smaller neighbouring countries, are seen as younger brothers to China's older brother. As younger brothers they should be respectful and in general supportive. One of the reasons that the relationship with Japan is frequently rocky is that Japan not only did not act as a younger brother in the past (invading China, taking over large parts of the country and killing millions of people) but continues not to act in that role in the present. Australia, on the other hand, tends to have good relations precisely because it does tend to act as a younger brother should.

Another source of irritation is the West's campaign on Human Rights. This is not to argue that gross violations of Human Rights do not take place in China: they do. However, many nationalists resent what they see as interference in Chinese affairs, a situation which translates as lack of respect for China. If it is possible to credit a country with face, then nationalists experience such criticism as infringing both the country's involvement face (in the sense of being seen as a good international citizen) and its independence face (in the sense of being left to pursue its own course without outside interference). In addition, many do not credit the good faith of western countries in general and the United States in particular in pointing to human rights violations. They point to the discrimination suffered by people of colour in the United States, and the tremendous poverty that exists in the richest country in the world, and draw parallels between Tibet and Hawaii and Alaska. As a result they tend to dismiss criticisms of China's human rights record as motivated by a desire to keep China from its rightful place.

Given the modern history of China, it is not surprising that strong national feelings are easily evoked, and that perceived slights result in strong reactions. Certain intellectuals also fear the effects of entry into the World Trade Organisation (WTO), believing that this will lock China into the position of supplier of cheap labour for factories producing goods destined for western consumers. They point out that the foreign companies that are moving their production facilities into China do so only because of China's low-cost environment. They charge that such companies repatriate their profits and make little or no effort to transfer technological skills and know-how, meaning that China has very little to gain from such operations. Such arguments enjoy not inconsiderable public support, and serve as a reminder that nationalist sentiments are never far from the surface. In this, China is not alone, as the ongoing appeal of Pauline Hanson's brand of narrow and xenophobic nationalism in Australia attests.

So far this discussion has centred on some of the more negative aspects of attitudes towards foreigners. Of equal importance are the positive aspects, many of which are related to the twin concepts of development and modernisation. The West in general and the United States in particular are admired for their achievements in science and technology. There is a widespread belief that in order to modernise and assume her rightful place in the world, China needs to develop her own scientific potential and acquire the most advanced technology available. This admiration is reflected in the extremely high numbers of students who elect to study science, engineering and information technology. It is also reflected in the large numbers of students who go abroad to pursue postgraduate studies in these areas in countries such as Australia, Germany, France, Japan, the United Kingdom and the United States.

'Inner' and 'outer' relationships

In the discussion on the expression of emotions (Chapter 6, page 91), we have already referred to the twin concepts of 'inner' and 'outer'. The distinction between inner and outer relationships runs through all Chinese relationships, starting with the family. For example, the paternal *zufu*, 'grandfather', and *zumu*, 'grandmother' contrasts with *waizufu*, 'maternal grandfather' and *waizumu*, 'maternal grandmother', *wai* meaning 'outside' or 'external'. At the other end of the scale, non-Chinese are *waiguoren*, literally 'external country people'. While I was teaching in Shanghai, I constantly heard people refer to the peasants who came into Shanghai to shop as *waidiren*, 'outside place people'.

The difference between inner and outer relationships is important because inner relationships are rule governed: that is, they are characterised by politeness, consideration and generally cordial and helpful attitudes. Outer relations are characterised by the opposite and are basically ungoverned. However, the contrast is not between two stark positions, because the inner relationship is graduated, its most intimate expression being within the family circle. Relationships between friends, between colleagues and between business associates are all characterised as inner, but to different degrees. The closer and more intimate the inner relationship is, the more the formal politeness that governs inner interactions is replaced by informality and by a directness that can sound abrupt to Australian ears.

While from one point of view, inner and outer relationships are fixed, in that a foreigner is always a foreigner, just as a maternal grandmother is always a maternal grandmother, from another point of view the boundary between inner and outer (and between gradations of inner) is constantly being negotiated. In other words, a person may be outer from one point of view, but inner from another. For example, foreigners are by definition outer from one point of view, but can establish inner relationships through work or study among other things. The relationship between a foreign manager and his or her Chinese colleagues will be an inner relationship when viewed from the company perspective, while remaining outer from the national perspective. Similarly, the relationship between colleagues in the same branch of a company is more inner than the relationship with people in other branches of the company.

The 'inner/outer' distinction helps to explain the contrast between public and private behaviour that many foreigners have noted. Relationships in public places such as bus stops and train stations are classified as outer relationships and so a great deal of pushing and shoving takes place in getting on a bus or train. Once on a train, however, inner relations can be gradually established by virtue of the shared carriage, and friendliness re-emerges. (The same cannot be said of buses, perhaps because of the shortness of the journeys.) Likewise, many people ignore road rules and traffic lights. The prevalence of litter especially in provincial towns and villages can also be understood in these terms. (Heavy fines and squads of cleaners have reduced its incidence in major cities.)

As noted in Chapter 6, page 91, the expression of negative emotions is strongly discouraged in inner relationships. This means that the open expression of anger, for example, may signal not only displeasure but also a change in relationship from inner to outer, with all the consequences that such a move entails. A great deal of repair work may be necessary to overcome such a breach, particularly as anger can also pose a major challenge to the involvement face that we discussed above. Australians need to keep in mind that it may therefore be difficult to re-establish relationships after an angry outburst. If anger is directed at them, they may also need to examine the situation closely in order to identify the factors that caused reclassification of the relationship from inner to outer.

Social relations

In formal analysis, Chinese Marxists divide society into two major groups: the propertied and the propertyless classes. Within these groups subdivisions are recognised. However, the informal division of society into various classes that prevail among most city-dwelling Chinese does not totally correspond to official analysis and it is the latter that will be discussed here.

Within the cities, most people recognise two broad divisions, roughly corresponding to the western division between 'white collar' and 'blue collar' occupations. White collar workers are generally regarded as further divided into several groups. The most interesting, from the Australian point of view, are intellectuals and public servants or *ganbu*. Countrywide, intellectuals comprise those who have graduated from high school, but within the cities people who have a tertiary education are generally considered to be intellectuals. The word 'intellectual' thus has a far wider meaning than it does in English. Intellectuals are considered to form a group within society and to have interests as a group. In the past, and particularly during the Cultural Revolution, they were also persecuted as a group.

After suffering from poor living conditions and low salaries during the 1980s and early 1990s, the conditions for many intellectuals, and especially for teachers and medical professionals, have improved markedly. They are not faced with the prospect of unemployment, as is the case with many workers, and salaries have greatly increased. In the case of those in the medical field, this is often the result of the introduction of 'user pays' principles, while the status and remuneration of teachers have risen as a result of increasing competition for tertiary places.

Ganbu form another distinct social group. *Ganbu* comprise those who work in an administrative capacity in government and party organisations. At the lower end of the scale, clerks and other such workers are included, but the scale stretches to the highest administrative positions in the country. In the past, *ganbu* exercised control over the daily life of every citizen and while this control has greatly decreased in recent years, they are still in a position to control the seals of approval which are needed to set up a business, for example, or to build a house.

Workers form the second major group in society. Until recently, industrial workers employed by state-owned enterprises enjoyed lifetime employment, relatively high wages, heavily subsidised housing, free health care and so on. For many, this is now a thing of the past. Reform of the state sector has seen the closure of many factories and the rationalisation of others. Middle-aged workers have born the brunt of this change: millions have lost their jobs and many have little if any chance of finding new ones.

At the same time, cities have seen a huge influx of rural workers who have taken positions in the new export-oriented industries located along China's coast. Most of these workers are young, and many of them female. Such young women also provide restaurants and hotels with their staff, and may find themselves working 14 to 16 hours a day without any holidays or days off. Their male counterparts have taken on the difficult, dirty and dangerous jobs that most urban dwellers refuse to perform; primarily jobs in the construction industry. Such workers have no security, no benefits and are frequently exploited by their employers and harassed by police. Moves in 2003 to simplify procedures for obtaining documents allowing them to work legally in cities will hopefully result in a diminution of such harassment.

Peasants constitute the third major grouping in Chinese society and comprise 50 per cent of the workforce. In fact, the agricultural sector is seriously overstaffed by world standards, and it remains to be seen how the sector will stand up to the competitive pressures unleashed by China's entry into the WTO. While it is true that the majority of peasants work on the land, an increasing number work in rural towns, in factories established by local authorities. However, these workers are still officially classified as peasants, as indeed are the construction workers and other migratory labourers of peasant origin who work in the cities. Whether a person is or is not a peasant tends to depend on where they live rather than the work that they do. Many peasants living near large cities and towns are comparatively wealthy, but the vast majority continue to live in poor conditions. Their sons and daughters provide the cheap labour on which the current spectacular growth of light industry depends.

Independent small businesspeople or *getihu* form another sector of the workforce, one that has expanded enormously over the last two decades. *Getihu* run small restaurants and shops, and perform a wide range of maintenance tasks such as bicycle repair, house painting, carpentry and so on. They run stalls in markets and help factories, even state factories, locate sources of scarce material. In short, they provide a very wide range of services and provide opportunities for people who would otherwise be unemployed to find a job.

At the other end of the scale, an independent professional class comprising businesspeople, accountants, lawyers, IT professionals and the like form the core of the emerging middle class. The class, centred in the great coastal cities such as Shanghai, Guangzhou, Tianjin and so on is increasingly important in forming public opinion, and is set to continue expanding in the foreseeable future.

While divisions between these various groups are considerably more fluid than they used to be, some differences remain difficult to overcome. Peasants, for example, may become factory workers, but it is much more difficult for them to become intellectuals or professionals. To move down the scale tends to involve great loss of face.

Differing popular conceptions of the way society is divided into classes and of how these classes relate to each other may give rise to a number of problems when Chinese come to Australia. Australians tend to divide society roughly into working class, middle class and upper class, with most classifying themselves as middle class. The existence, however, of a strong egalitarian ethic means that the divisions are relatively fluid and that transition from one group to another happens relatively easily. In addition, many would deny that such divisions exist at all and almost all would agree that judgments of social desirability or acceptability based on class distinctions are invalid.

Chinese arriving in Australia would first of all be unfamiliar not only with Australian class divisions, but crucially with their fluidity. On arrival, many Chinese are forced to find employment as workers, while in China they may have been white collar workers – intellectuals, for example. Many regard this as a serious loss of face and may attempt to apologise for their work, or even to hide their present occupation from Australian friends.

Many will be puzzled by the Australian emphasis on egalitarianism. Australian university graduates who willingly engage in manual labour or, even more strangely, voluntarily move to the countryside are likely to be regarded incredulously.

Some may ascribe to Australian public servants the powers exercised by Chinese *ganbu,* and more seriously may seek back doors through which to influence their decisions. When such back doors fail to materialise, as usually happens, this may be ascribed to the seeker's lack of familiarity with Australian back doors rather than to the fact that back doors are rather less common in Australia than they are in China. Others may approach people they know, such as teachers, for special favours, and may feel that the teacher is being unreasonable in not cooperating.

Finally, most Chinese are at least initially likely to equate rural conditions in China and Australia and to ascribe to rural dwellers in Australia a level of deprivation that even in times of economic difficulty does not exist.

Classroom Tasks

■ TASK 1 ■

Values clarification

Answer this questionnaire for yourself, and then ask an equal number of Chinese and Australians to complete it. Collate the answers obtained by everyone in the class. Are there any major differences between the answers typically given by Chinese and those typically given by Australians? What similarities are there in the answers?

Read the following statements and state whether you agree or disagree with them, using the following scale:

1 = strongly agree   **2** = agree   **3** = neutral   **4** = disagree   **5** = strongly disagree

	1	2	3	4
1. A group needs to have a leader otherwise it will not function effectively.				
2. It is natural and desirable for people to marry.				

	1	2	3	4
3. People should control nature in order to improve their quality of life.				
4. If people do not respect authority society will suffer.				
5. Teenagers should obey their parents because parents are more experienced.				
6. If individual desires conflict with the needs of the family, then the individual should give way.				
7. Friendship has no place in business.				
8. The past has a strong influence on the future.				
9. A person should make their own decisions uninfluenced by others.				
10. Because of human nature there will always be war.				

■ TASK 2 ■

Waltzing Matilda is the best known of all Australian songs, and is Australia's unofficial national anthem.

Read the words to the song, and answer the questions that follow.

What does the song tell you about Australian attitudes?

Waltzing Matilda

Once a jolly swagman sat by a billabong
Under the shade of a coolibah tree
And he sang as he sat and waited till his billy boiled
You'll come a'waltzing, Matilda, with me.

Chorus:

Waltzing Matilda, waltzing Matilda,
You'll come a'waltzing Matilda with me
And he sang as he sat and waited till his billy boiled
You'll come a'waltzing, Matilda with me.

Down came a jumbuck to drink at the billabong
Up jumped the swagman and grabbed him with glee
And he sang as he stuffed that jumbuck in his tuckerbag
You'll come a'waltzing, Matilda, with me.

swagman: a tramp who walks from farm to farm looking for work.
billabong: small pond, lake.
billy: a pot for boiling water on a fire.

Matilda: The swagman's swag, a rolled-up blanket that contains everything the swagman owns. 'Waltzing Matilda' means that the swagman is alone and only has his swag to dance with.

jumbuck: a male sheep.

tuckerbag: a bag used to hold food.

Chorus

Down came the squatter mounted on his thoroughbred Up came the troopers, one, two, three Where's that jolly jumbuck you've got in your tuckerbag? You'll come a'waltzing, Matilda, with me. Up jumped the swagman and jumped into the billabong 'You'll never catch me alive,' said he And his ghost may be heard as you pass by that billabong You'll come a'waltzing, Matilda, with me. Chorus	**squatter:** a rich farmer. **troopers:** soldiers.

a. Why was the swagman sitting by the billabong?

b. Why did he steal the sheep?

c. What did the squatter do?

d. Why did the swagman commit suicide?

e. Do you think this song represents Australian values and attitudes? If so, what values and attitudes does it represent?

Choose a song that you think represents China and Chinese values.

a. Explain the meaning of the song to your teacher.

b. What values and attitudes do you think this song represents?

c. Compare the values of *Waltzing Matilda* with the values displayed in the song that you chose.

■ TASK 3 ■

Proverbs often illustrate the important values of a culture. Below are ten well-known English proverbs.

Read the proverbs and check the meaning of any that you don't understand. (Use your dictionary or ask your teacher.)

a. Which of these ten proverbs do you think most represent Australian attitudes? Why?

b. Which do you think least represent Australian attitudes? Why?

1. Time is money

2. The squeaky wheel gets the grease

3. Look before you leap

4. While the cat's away the mice will play

5. A stitch in time saves nine

6. You can't put an old head on young shoulders

7. Many hands make light work

8. Every cloud has a silver lining

9. He who hesitates is lost

10. A bird in the hand is worth two in the bush

Now choose five Chinese proverbs that you think best represent important Chinese values.

a. Explain their meaning in English.

b. Compare your choice with the choices of others in the class.

c. Explain why you chose these proverbs.

■ TASK 4 ■

Look at a set of Australian banknotes and identify the figures on each side of each note.

a. Find out about the achievements of each person depicted.

b. Why were these people selected to be shown on banknotes?

c. What can you learn about Australian attitudes and values from the figures on banknotes?

(**NB:** The Reserve Bank of Australia's website gives useful information about Australian banknotes. http://www.rba.gov.au/CurrencyNotes/NotesInCirculation)

Now look at what is depicted on Chinese banknotes.

a. Describe the figures on Chinese banknotes and explain why they were chosen.

b. What do the figures on Chinese banknotes tell you about Chinese attitudes and values?

■ TASK 5 ■

Choose one object that you think best represents an important aspect of Chinese culture, and one object that you think best represents an important aspect of Australian culture.

Compare your choices with those of other students in the class.

Why did you choose your two objects?

What does each object represent?

■ TASK 6 ■

Below is a table showing maximum punishments for various crimes in several countries.

a. Working in pairs, fill in the line for China.

b. Which country has the fairest punishments? Why?

c. Which country has the least fair punishments? Why?

Country/State	Crime				
	Murder	Rape	Armed robbery	Tax fraud	Assault
NSW	Life	20 years	20 years	10 years	25 years
Canada	Life	Life	5 years	18 months	4 years
Denmark	Life	3 years	6 years	10 months	1 year
England	Life	15 years	14 years	3 years	5 years
Germany	Life	10 years	10 years	10 years	5 years
Texas	Death	50 years	99 years	99 years	10 years
Kenya	Death	Life	Death	3 years	Life
China					

■ TASK 7 ■

Almost all court cases in Australia are open – anyone can go and watch.

Your research task is to go and watch an Australian court for two or three hours. Your teacher will help you find out where to go.

Before you go, find out what each of the following people do:

a. the judge

b. the jury

c. the defendant

d. the defence lawyer(s)

e. the prosecution lawyer(s)

f. the clerk of the court

g. the witness.

After you have attended the court, answer the following questions:

a. Draw a diagram of the court showing where each of the seven people mentioned above sit.

b. What crime was the defendant accused of?

c. Did he/she plead guilty or not guilty?

d. How many witnesses were there?

e. What did the jury decide?

f. If he/she was convicted, what was his/her punishment?

g. If he/she had been convicted in China, what might his/her punishment have been? Compare your answers to those of others in the class.

■ TASK 8 ■

Robert was the manager of a large computing company and was advertising for a computer programmer. One night at home he received a telephone call from a friend, Liu Dongping, who came from Shanghai. Liu Dongping said that he was interested in the job. Robert told him to send a copy of his curriculum vitae. Liu sent the copy and two days later rang up to check that it had arrived. Robert said that it had, but he didn't sound very pleased. Liu didn't understand why, but thought it might be because Robert was busy.

A few days later Liu was asked to an interview with Robert and after the interview he was quite confident. When he found out that he had not in fact got the job, he was shocked, angry and hurt. He felt that Robert had betrayed him and decided to break off his friendship.

Why didn't Liu Dongping get the job?

Was he correct in deciding to break off his friendship with Robert?

What would you advise Liu Dongping to do in future?

Notes

1 The definition which follows is based on Scollon, R., & Scollon, S. W. (1995). *Intercultural communication.* Oxford: Blackwell, Chapter 3.
2 The following discussion is based on Yang, Mayfair M. H. (1994). *Gifts, favors and banquets: The art of social relationships in China.* Ithaca, NY: Cornell University Press, an illuminating academic study.
3 Nathan, A., & Gilley, B. (Eds.). (2002). *China's new rulers: The secret files.* New York: Granta, p 191.

CHAPTER EIGHT

DOING BUSINESS IN CHINA

In doing business in China, it is important to remember that conditions are not uniform. The situation in coastal Shanghai, which is self-confident, modern, cosmopolitan and entrepreneurial, is very different from the situation in inland Chongqing, which is only just beginning major reform and opening. It is different again in the rust-bucket cities of the north-east, cities like Shenyang, which were centres of heavy industry and which have born the brunt of the closures and unemployment that have accompanied the reform process, without necessarily having seen many of the benefits. In reading what follows, it is essential to take notice of local conditions: more than one business has failed through approaching China and its market as a whole.

As this chapter is largely concerned with the ways that the common Chinese attitudes and values are expressed in business practice, it is useful to have read Chapter 7 before embarking on this.

Names and business cards

We discussed the ways in which Chinese names are organised in Chapter 4, page 33. It is important to remember that the Chinese equivalent of the given name is rarely used except in intimate circumstances, so it is appropriate when speaking to a Chinese associate to use their title and family name, or their title and full name on first meeting. Some Chinese select an English first name in order to give English speakers a friendly way of addressing them without the embarrassment which would accompany the use of the Chinese given name.

By the same token, many foreign business people adopt a Chinese name, a practice which not only assists those Chinese who have difficulty in pronouncing English names but also indicates interest in Chinese culture. Basically, there are two common ways of selecting a name. Firstly, the English name can be transliterated using Chinese characters which have approximately the same sound. For example, Harry Potter becomes *Ha li Bo te*. Selection is not, however, a simple procedure. Careless selection of characters can result in unfortunate renderings. The experience of the Coca-Cola Company is a case in point. Their first attempt to render Coca-Cola into Chinese resulted in *ke kou ke le*, but the characters selected translated as 'Bite the wax tadpole'. After furious activity and a large number of shredded publicity handouts, a new set of characters was selected having the wonderfully propitious meaning 'Pleasure in the mouth'.

Another problem with direct transliteration is that the resulting Chinese form may be rather unwieldy. If the name is simple, as in Bush, for example, this is not a problem: the form is *Bu she*. However, a name like Rumsfeld presents greater problems: *La mu si fei er de* is a quite a mouthful in Chinese!

A more appropriate way is to select a name comprising three characters: that is, a Chinese-style name, using characters that sound somewhat similar to the English name. This procedure will give several different possibilities. Here are some, based on my own name, Jean Brick:

Bi Jiang
Bai Zhi ning
Bai Jiao ning
Bei Zhao ning

In each case, a standard Chinese family name is used, based on the 'B' sound in my family name. Various characters have been selected to approximate the sound of my given name, but care has been taken to ensure a pleasant meaning.

A further alternative would be to use *Zhen* for my given name. This is the standard translation of Jane, and few Chinese can hear the difference between Jean and Jane. There are in fact standard forms for a number of the more common English names; for example, David is *Da wei* and Mary is *Ma li*. These can be used, but often they do not fit into the standard three character form of most Chinese names.

However, choosing a Chinese name is a skill. Don't try it at home! In order to ensure that you have an appropriate Chinese name which creates a good impression, it is advisable to ask a native speaker of Chinese with a good education to choose it. This way unpleasant surprises will be avoided.

The same goes for the translation of company names and slogans. We have already mentioned the Coca-Cola experience. Pepsi had a similar experience, with their slogan 'Come alive with the Pepsi generation' being rendered 'Pepsi will bring your Ancestors back from the dead'.

Business cards are essential, and serve, in a hierarchically ordered society, to indicate not only a person's name but also the position held in the company, so it is important to make sure that this information is prominently displayed. Ideally, a business card will use English on one side and Chinese on the other, but as always, the cardinal rule is to get an educated native speaker of Chinese to check the wording before printing. Large numbers of cards tend to be needed, because they are presented to everyone, and by the same token large numbers are collected, and constitute a vital resource bank as they may later form the basis for the development of a *guanxi* relationship.

Business cards are presented with both hands. When a card is presented, it should be read carefully, and then placed on the table for ease of reference if in a meeting, or into a card holder. It is impolite to glance at it, put it in a wallet and put the wallet in a back pocket: such actions indicate disrespect.

Look at any Chinese business card that you have been given.

a. Identify the family name and the given name on the card.

b. What is the title of this person?

c. How would you address this person?

d. What other information do the card give?

e. Compare the information on this card with the information on your own card. Does the comparison suggest any changes that you might make to your own Chinese business card?

Maintaining face in business relationships

In Chapter 7, we defined face as the public image that each participant in an interaction wants to project about him or herself and the image that each grants the other. In other words, face is concerned with how we want others to see us, and with how we allow others to present themselves to us. This means that we not only have face ourselves, but we also give face to others.

Before we explore what this means in practice, it is important also to remember that face has two aspects: involvement face, which has to do with our desire to be seen as useful and contributing members of society, and independence face, which involves our desire to maintain our personal independence and freedom of action, and to grant others similar freedom of action.

To find out how important face is to Australians, imagine yourself occupying a senior managerial or technical position in a company, and suddenly finding all your decisions and every piece of your correspondence subject to review and ratification by those senior to yourself. Most Australians would find such close oversight extremely unpleasant, and for many it would result in resignation and a new job. This is because Australians tend to place great emphasis on their independence face, although they are not likely to regard it as face: they are more likely to regard it as the natural order of things.

In the same way, most Chinese are very sensitive to threats to their involvement face, and they too tend to regard concern with this aspect of face as the natural order of things. We can go further and say that because of their sensitivity to independence face, many Australians will interpret threats to that face as deliberate. In the same way, Chinese may interpret threats to their involvement face as deliberate. This may be so within the context of each culture, but when Chinese and Australians interact with each other, it is more likely that threats to each other's face are unintentional, and are the result of lack of understanding.

In practice, different approaches to face have important consequences. Here, we will briefly examine its importance in relation to hierarchically organised workplaces, to issues of responsibility and to criticism.

Most Chinese workplaces are hierarchically organised, with power and decision-making centralised at the top and carefully demarcated levels and responsibilities below. When Australians enter into joint venture partnerships with Chinese companies, often one of the first things that they try to do is to give greater responsibility to people at various levels of the organisation. In attempting this, they frequently encounter a great deal of resistance, and may conclude that Chinese lack initiative. In fact, what they fail to realise is that by attempting to increase a subordinate's freedom of action, they are placing the subordinate in a position which is likely to result in infringement of the involvement face of his or her superiors. Resistance is therefore not surprising, and difficult to overcome within the context of a joint venture. If the venture is wholly Australian-owned, the situation is easier, because management is able to model and support devolution of authority, and thus valorise independence and independence face. It is also able to build trust through activities aimed at strengthening relationships, such as banquets, staff picnics and other outings. However, it is important to remember that changing deeply embedded cultural attitudes is a slow process, and that even in situations where a company's culture strongly supports independence, many Chinese staff members are likely to be slow to fully adapt to its demands.

Different understandings of the importance of face are also closely related to the concept of responsibility. The Australian and more broadly the western approach is to vest responsibility primarily in the individual. Furthermore, when mistakes are made, the responsible individual is usually identified in the effort to find the cause of the error and to prevent a repetition.

In the Chinese situation, it is far more likely that effort will be devoted to repairing damage rather than to establishing individual or even corporate responsibility, which obviously has the potential to be seriously face threatening. Indeed, when forced by foreign partners to identify responsibility, it is likely that there will be a resort to delaying tactics and obfuscation. Action taken to repair damage may be indirect. Blackman[1] discusses the case of a wine press that was broken in the course of being transported from port to winery. Australian attempts to establish responsibility met with evasion, denial of responsibility and outright fabrication. The situation was, however, resolved in the following way. A new press was supplied, and over the following 18 months the company received favourable treatment from the customs authorities, so that all losses were covered.

In the same vein, criticism and correction is normally given indirectly rather than directly, and often in general rather than specific terms. Those being criticised are thus given the opportunity to improve their performance without incurring a catastrophic loss of face.

What actions by senior management in your company would cause you to consider seeking another position?

a. Can you relate these actions to the concept of independence face outlined above?

b. How would the actions you have identified leave you feeling?

What type of actions might infringe your involvement face?

How might you react to such actions?

What implications do these different concepts of face have for doing business in China?

Developing relationships

In Chapter 7, page 107, we examined two related concepts, *renqing* and *guanxi*. *Renqing* refers to the natural feeling of affection and interdependence that exists between people, and *guanxi* to the instrumentalisation of that feeling: the use of relationships to achieve specific ends. These two concepts play a vital role in business. The role of the first is illustrated in the following experience.

A good friend of mine is a Chinese-born businessman now resident in Australia. His company does a great deal of business with Chinese companies, and consequently often plays host to senior management from these companies. On these occasions, he meets the team (and it is always a team, rather than an individual) at the airport and drives them to their hotel. The enjoyment and wellbeing of the team then becomes his sole focus of attention for the duration of their visit. He may drive them up to the Gold Coast for a couple of days, or to Canberra to see the sights of the capital. He takes them to whatever entertainment venues they are interested in, from Kings Cross and the casino to the Opera House and Taronga Park Zoo, and wines them and dines them every evening at good restaurants. Some time in the visit may be devoted to visiting business sites (factories, building sites, and so on) or to meeting senior management of other companies involved or proposing involvement in the business venture concerned, but such activities will occupy quite a small amount of the time available. Business may not even be broached during the first couple of days of the visit. When serious discussions do start, it is not in the context of a formal meeting, but over a meal, or during a trip. Decisions reached informally may or may not be endorsed during the course of a formal meeting: if non-Chinese partners are involved, a formal meeting is more likely.

In undertaking such extensive hospitality, what my friend is displaying is the fact that he understands and possesses proper human feeling. Both he and his guests are developing and maintaining the warm personal relationship which is considered to be the basis of a successful business relationship. It should be remembered that historically, Chinese law did not cover commercial transactions, meaning that the sentiment 'my word is my bond' had a depth and importance in many ways greater than that involved in the English concept. While China is rapidly developing a large body of commercial law, it will be some time before that law is invested with the same bedrock quality that characterises commercial law in the West. It is not surprising, then, that relationship is so important in the Chinese business context.

Many Australian companies tend to underestimate the importance of devoting time to developing close relationships. This is typified by the very short amounts of time put aside for face-to-face negotiation of contracts: the fly in, discuss, sign, fly out model. When such negotiations encounter problems, they tend to attribute all responsibility to the Chinese. However, companies that have invested time and effort in establishing good relations tend to encounter fewer problems precisely because the time previously invested is translated into trust.

Companies that have a long history of doing business in China are seen as reliable and not likely to pull out in difficult times. They have in effect displayed that they understand the imperatives of *renqing* and as a result are trusted partners, and they may find themselves offered a wide range of opportunities, some of which may be outside their areas of expertise. Expertise is in many cases seen as less important than relationships.

Other examples which illustrate a lack of understanding of the need to develop relationships include the perception that banqueting and other such entertainment are a waste of time. One large Australian mining company received a visit from an important Chinese delegation, but none of the senior management was able to spare the time to either brief them or to join them at dinner. While the Chinese delegation involved made no comment at the time, it was noticeable that the subsequent negotiations dragged on far longer than was the norm.

Australians may also underestimate the importance of showing their consideration for all members of the workforce by arranging and participating in social activities involving the whole workforce. Such activities include day outings to nearby scenic spots and weekend trips to famous tourist destinations. Within the context of the hierarchical and paternal nature of Chinese superior-subordinate relations, such events serve to demonstrate senior management's *renqing* and so build trust.

Guanxi builds on and extends *renqing* in an instrumental fashion, as discussed in Chapter 7. *Guanxi* ties are based on a number of different relationships. Ties of family and friendship are important, as are those with neighbours. The sharing of common origins, that is, common village, town or even province can be important, as can shared experience. Having been to school or university together creates lasting bonds that can be incorporated into a *guanxi* network, as can shared military experience or, for the Chinese equivalent of baby-boomers, the experience of being sent together down to the countryside in the Cultural Revolution.

Within Chinese companies there is often a group of people who have wide *guanxi* networks and who use these networks to facilitate company business. These networks are personal and cannot be taken over by another person unless that person is deliberately introduced to all participants in the network. In many cases, company salespeople rely on *guanxi* networks to sell their goods, while others use their networks to source needed supplies and raw materials.

Guanxi ties can be called upon to facilitate an enormous range of interactions. These include transactions with bureaucracy, where the personal introduction provided by the *guanxi* relationship is likely to simplify procedures for obtaining the permits and chops (the functional equivalent of signatures) that are needed for almost every enterprise.

The *guanxi* relationship can also assist in making contact with the right people, that is, with the people who have decision-making power in specific areas. Such people may be difficult to contact without a personal introduction, but may also be essential in enabling business to proceed.

Guanxi ties can also be important in ensuring the smooth functioning of services such as rubbish collections or even access to reliable supplies of electricity and water. This applies especially in smaller cities and towns in less developed areas.

In the light of the discussion on relationship in this and the previous chapter, how might you go about:

- developing a relationship with a company with which you have not previously done business

- maintaining a relationship with a company that you presently do business with?

One area in which the importance of relationship is likely to clash with western ideas regarding efficiency and best practice is that of procurement. Many Chinese businesses prefer to source raw materials, supplies and so on with companies with whom they have previously done business – that is, where a relationship exists. This preference will frequently outweigh the issue of quality, and has been known to cause problems in many joint ventures.

Task-based and relationship-based approaches to business

The concepts of face and relationship are clearly reflected in the way that people judge their effectiveness in a business context. This can be seen in the results of a survey of a number of wholly owned and joint venture companies, carried out under the auspices of the Victorian Branch of the Australia China Business Council by the University of Melbourne's Jane Orton.[2] The survey investigated the ways in which Australian and Chinese employees of these companies regarded themselves and the ways in which they regarded each other. Broadly speaking, the Australians identified attributes related to the ability to carry out a task while the Chinese focused on attributes likely to contribute to the development of successful relationships. The Chinese thus saw themselves as warm, friendly and cooperative, and Australians as friendly, polite, generous, helpful and easy to get on with. The Australians, on the other hand, saw themselves as single-minded, determined and decisive, and as leaders who were keen to be successful. They saw their Chinese counterparts as intelligent, hardworking, open-minded, inquisitive, knowledge-starved and enthusiastic.

This difference was also seen in the negative characteristics that each group identified in their counterparts. The Australians saw the Chinese as indecisive, cautious, procrastinating and as using a different logic, while the Chinese saw the Australians as poor at *guanxi*, reluctant to share power and arrogant.

This is not to argue that Australians ignore relationship-building completely, or that Chinese are not in any way task-oriented. In fact, Australians tended to identify their own weaknesses in relational terms (arrogant, aggressive, intolerant and insensitive), while Chinese focused on their task-oriented weaknesses (unenterprising and avoiding responsibility).

Such differences in approach can be a source of strength if they are used appropriately, but also have the potential to give rise to a self-reinforcing negative spiral if considered in isolation. In other words, one of the keys to successful business development in China is to value and utilise relationships as much as efficiency, competition and best practice are valued in Australia.

Think about your performance in the position that you occupy.

a. Evaluate your own performance in this position, identifying three or four strong points and a similar number of weak points.

b. What criteria did you use to make these judgments?

c. How do your judgments relate to the task-related orientation identified above?

d. What implications does your own orientation to your job have for possible interactions with Chinese colleagues?

Banquets

Formal banquets are an important part of building and maintaining business relationships. Generally, any business trip to China will result in at least one banquet, and probably two: one given by the Chinese side and the other by the Australian side. The same applies when Chinese business people are visiting Australia.

A Chinese banquet can be either enjoyable or an ordeal, depending largely on the state of mind in which it is approached. The most important thing to remember is that it is not a waste of time, quite the reverse, in fact. Banquets not only contribute to relationship building, they also allow business issues to be thrashed out informally.

Banquets are usually held in a private room in a well-known restaurant or hotel. Guests will be seated around a circular table, with the host sitting in the seat immediately opposite the door and the highest-ranking guest, that is, the guest of honour, sitting on his left. Seating is strictly hierarchical with the host indicating where each guest should sit. However, because modesty is a highly valued trait, a Chinese guest of honour may initially decline to take the place of honour. In this case, the host gently but firmly insists and after two or three polite attempts to decline, the guest will accept. It is appropriate for an Australian guest of honour to behave the same way. Similarly, Australian hosts should ensure that they are thoroughly familiar with the relative status or seniority of all their guests.

Each place is normally set with a small bowl sitting on a plate, a pair of chopsticks resting on a small chopstick holder and two or three glasses. The smallest glass is used for spirits. The larger glasses are used for soft drinks, beer or wine. A serviette will also be provided.

Regarding the use of chopsticks, if you are not familiar with them, then it is advisable to learn. While knives and forks may be available in the larger cities, they are unlikely to be in smaller places. Also, using chopsticks sends a subtle signal about a person's familiarity with and acceptance of Chinese customs, and therefore contributes to the all-important development of relationship. When chopsticks are not being used, they are placed on the chopstick holder provided. They should not be placed across the bowl as this is impolite. Even more importantly, they should not be stuck upright in the bowl of rice. This is reminiscent of the way that sticks of incense are offered to the dead and is both impolite and unlucky.

Generally speaking, a traditional banquet starts with a number of small cold snacks, including dishes such as cold chicken, boiled peanuts, thousand-year-eggs[3] and preserved fish. These dishes will be on the table when guests are seated. The banquet starts when the host picks up his chopsticks, selects a morsel from one of the best dishes and places it in the bowl of the guest of honour. This is a signal for the other Chinese to do the same thing for the guests sitting beside them.

After a few minutes, hot dishes will be placed on the table. Guests may help themselves to any of these dishes, while the Chinese hosts will continue both to ply them with choice pieces and to urge them to eat more. As a typical banquet may involve anything from 15 to 30 different dishes, it is advisable not to eat too much too quickly.

It is not expected that all the food provided will be eaten: in fact, the host will have ordered far more than is needed. This is because to completely finish a dish indicates that insufficient was prepared and this in turn signifies that the host is tight-fisted. By the same token, a guest should not allow his dish to become empty as this indicates that he has not had enough, and by implication that not enough has been provided. Instead, a little is always left in the bottom of the bowl.

Usually common bowls are provided for bones, prawn shells and the like. Alternatively, each person may have a pile of bowls in front of them, one on top of another. In this case, the guest leaves any bones or shells in the topmost bowl, which is then removed, leaving the next bowl for the following course or courses.

Dishes are served in an order which is carefully designed to highlight differences in flavour, texture and colour, which means that sweet dishes are not kept to the end of the meal, but may be served at any time. In some areas, the end of the meal is signalled by the appearance of soup, usually followed by fruit. In others, several soups may be served during the course of the meal, in which case the last dish is likely to be a green vegetable, also followed by fruit. In most areas, staples such as rice, noodles or dumplings are offered just before the end of the meal. In the context of a banquet, these are regarded as fillers, and it is not expected that many guests would still be hungry enough to want them. They must however be offered.

Once the meal is finished, it is polite to leave quickly, and it is the responsibility of the senior guest to make the first move.

If you are offered a dish that you do not like, it is better to taste a small amount of it, rather than reject it outright. If however it is something that is really unpalatable, you can explain that you have an allergy or other medical condition that makes it inadvisable for you to eat it. The palatability problem works both ways: many Chinese find some western food as unpalatable as Australians find some Chinese dishes. This is particularly so of cheese and dishes involving cheese, steak and large cuts of rare meat, and cream sauces. Lamb in particular tends to be regarded with something close to disgust by many, the smell being regarded as overpowering. When Australians are hosting Chinese, it is often safer to choose a good Chinese restaurant for such an occasion, rather than risk unfamiliar foods.[4]

Perhaps the most difficult aspect of a banquet relates to alcohol. We noted above that several different glasses are provided. The smallest one is for spirits, which are used only for toasts. Soft drinks and wine or beer can be drunk throughout the meal and tea is also usually available.

Several minutes into the meal, the host will normally rise to propose the first toast. This should be followed a few minutes later by the guest of honour, who also proposes a toast. Other toasts will follow at intervals from people of progressively lower rank. Toasts will usually be offered to friendship between the two countries, to the deepening business relationship, to mutual benefit and to good health.

Things get complicated if, as sometimes happens, the banquet involves a drinking competition. Drinking competitions can serve to deepen a relationship but can also at times indicate a jockeying for power and position. What each particular drinking competition symbolises is something that can only be decided in relation to the context in which it occurs. One sign that a drinking competition is on the cards is when you are told in advance that so-and-so is a great drinker. In other cases, you may only realise what is going on once you get to the banquet. In either case, there are several options. Firstly, you can take up the challenge. In this case, be sure that you have a hard head: Chinese spirits are 50 per cent to 60 per cent proof, and toasts in drinking competitions involve draining the glass. If the ethos of the business in which you are involved is relatively masculine, then you may gain considerable kudos if you win. You are likely to establish your credentials as a tough and strong-minded negotiator. If, on the other hand, you lose, this loss may affect your business standing.

If you are reluctant to get involved, then, if possible, avoid going to a banquet alone. This means that the burden of offering and responding to multiple toasts can be shared around a group. If one of your team has a hard head, you can nominate this person to bear the brunt of the drinking. In this case, the comments made above apply.

There are, however, other strategies that you can adopt. Carolyn Blackman, in her book of case studies of business in China, relates the experience of one Australian businessman who, on being called upon to drink a toast, replied that he never drank alone. This ensured that the whole Chinese team had to drink each toast with him and prevented a situation in which he drank each toast while each of his Chinese counterparts drank only one.

You can also nominate someone to drink for you, a useful tactic if you are the only Australian, or you can drink all toasts in wine or beer. If so, it is useful to acknowledge that this is what you are doing, and possibly to make a joke of it to avoid any impression of aloofness. If you do not drink at all, you need to state this, and to explain it using a medical reason: other explanations too easily sound as if you are being reserved or even unfriendly.

Finally, *ganbei*, loosely translated as 'bottoms up', means that you should drain your glass. If you do not wish to do this, you may sip the toast instead, but again it is useful to indicate in a good-humoured manner that this is what you are going to do.

The situation for women is slightly different. Women are not usually challenged to drinking games, and run the risk of being perceived as overly aggressive if they participate in them successfully. The safest strategy is to politely indicate that you are not used to drinking large amounts of alcohol and to sip all toasts rather than drain the glass. You can also make use of the strategies outlined above.

All the above relates to traditional banquets, which are still by far the most prevalent outside great centres such as Shanghai. However, in Shanghai and some other more cosmopolitan centres, certain changes are taking place in traditional banqueting procedure. Firstly, it is increasingly common to find that large dishes are no longer placed in the centre of the table. Instead, each guest is served with a small amount of each dish. This means that during the course of a meal, a guest may be served with anything up to 15 or even 20 bowls. This makes it even more important that guests do not eat too much early in the meal. It is also important not to finish everything in each bowl.

Secondly, even if individual servings are not provided, serving spoons are replacing chopsticks as the means of placing food in individual bowls. In other words, it is becoming much rarer to see individuals use their own chopsticks to help themselves to a common dish or to place food in guests' bowls.

Whatever the circumstances, perhaps the best way to find out about banquets is to participate in one.

What difficulties do you think a meal at a smart Australian restaurant serving non-Chinese food might pose for Chinese?

How would you advise a Chinese colleague faced with, for example, a meal at a good Italian restaurant? What would he or she need to know?

How might these difficulties compare with the difficulties you might face with a Chinese banquet?

Negotiations

Chinese negotiators have a deserved reputation for driving a very hard bargain. This does not mean that the preferred option is 'win, lose', but it does mean that in securing a 'win, win' outcome, they are, not unnaturally, likely to prioritise the Chinese 'win'.

Negotiations may be held around a table, but may also take place in a large room with armchairs ranged around the room. Senior people should be chosen to represent the Australian company, as those in junior positions are unlikely to command enough respect to give credence to the negotiations. Young people, even those occupying senior positions, also operate at a disadvantage.

The process of negotiation may take rather longer than would be the case in Australia, especially if there is no previous history of relationship. In this case, the first meeting or meetings are likely to be devoted to relationship building, involving presentations about both companies, their histories, products and so on. Banquets and other social outings may well accompany this phase. As has been discussed above, many Australians are impatient with this procedure and attempt to 'expedite' business. In general, this will not only stress relations, but will also result in more delays further down the track.

Once serious negotiations commence, then every aspect of the proposed business is likely to be carefully scrutinised. It is important to be on top of all the fine detail of the proposal, and to be ready to answer a wide range of questions, many of which may occur more than once. It is useful to have as much material as possible to present in the form of tables, graphs and other visual representations, which helps to overcome language difficulties. Consistency is essential, as inconsistencies may be taken as indicative of bad faith. As boasting is viewed in a very negative light, claims should not be exaggerated and gung-ho presentations avoided.

Decisions are not usually reached within the confines of a business meeting. This is because Chinese decision-making power is normally concentrated at the top of the organisational ladder, and little of it is or can be delegated. Furthermore, the actual decision-maker may not participate in the negotiations at all, or if he (it is usually he) does so, his decision-making power may not be apparent. Negotiators therefore need to consult with decision-makers in private. In addition, before any decision can be made, a wide range of interests which would not normally be involved in an Australian business decision need to be consulted. These might include the municipal authorities, representatives from the power and the water authorities, and customs and tax representatives among others. All these interests need to be satisfied before negotiations can be finalised.

In all this, the need to maintain and give face is very important to both sides, but will be expressed in different ways. Australians may experience the intensive scrutiny of the proposal, and especially of its technical details, as questioning their technical expertise. They may also experience the protracted negotiation process – together with the demands of living in a hotel away from family, attending banquets and other social events, and having very little or no personal time – as inconsiderate, or even as a deliberate attempt to wear them down. All these acts constitute assaults on an Australian's sense of independence face, which involves the right to maintain autonomy and be free from the impositions of others.

Chinese, on the other hand, being more sensitive to assaults on involvement face, are likely to avoid giving direct answers, particularly if the answer is negative. Rather than present negative or difficult information, they are likely to procrastinate or to return indecisive answers. They are also responsible for obtaining a beneficial outcome for the Chinese party, and since failure to do so would involve a major loss of face, they are strongly motivated to drive a hard bargain.

In this situation, it is important to recognise that the need to maintain face is not an illogical peculiarity confined to Chinese, but is experienced by both parties, though in different ways. Failure to perceive this can place Australian companies at a disadvantage. For example, technical personnel can become so angry at the type of questioning they are subjected to in the course of negotiations that their efficiency is impaired and relationships with the Chinese seriously damaged.

Australian negotiators are usually outnumbered by their Chinese counterparts. This places additional strains upon them because they are often placed in situations where they need to assimilate a large amount of information and to decide on their line of response at the same time. The Chinese meanwhile have the possibility of delegating some team members to take careful notes while others formulate responses. Australians should be ready to call for time out when they feel that this is appropriate.

Finally, it is important to remain polite and calm even in the face of provocation. This may well be a tactic aimed at putting the Australian team off balance. Even if it is not, response in kind is likely to cause more loss of face to the Australians than it is to the Chinese. One of the best pieces of advice I received on my first visit to China more than 20 years ago was that I could lose my temper just once, but that it should not be until I had developed a reputation for calmness and politeness; in other words, it should not be until I had developed an inner relationship. Even then, it was to be the result of a rational decision and not an action taken in the heat of the moment. Under such circumstances, it could serve to develop an even closer relationship (keeping in mind that close inner relationships allow for the more direct expression of emotion). Otherwise, it could precipitate a redefinition of the relationship in terms of outer rather than inner, and entail a long and painful process to restore harmony and understanding. It was good advice.

Commercial law and contracts

We have already seen (Chapter 7, page 114) that the Chinese attitude to law is particularistic rather than universal, with the central authorities passing laws that are interpreted by local authorities in the light of current conditions. While this approach at times opens the door on corruption, it also recognises the difficulty of legislating for a country as vast and varied as China. However, recent years have seen attempts to limit local powers, and these attempts have been strengthened with China's joining the World Trade Organisation (WTO). This does not yet mean, however, that regional and local variation in the application of laws and regulations is a thing of the past. For this reason, and because *guanxi* relationships have a strong local flavour, businesses often find it useful to establish regionally rather than nationally based distribution systems, as this allows them the flexibility to respond to the conditions prevailing in different regions.

The recent origins of China's commercial law also mean that it has not yet developed the absolute and impartial authority that it enjoys in western countries. As a result, commercial undertakings which are regarded as binding in Australia may not be seen in the same light in China. A case in point is that of the contract. Contracts drawn up by Chinese companies tend to be fairly short and general in their wording when compared to those drawn up by Australian companies. This reflects a somewhat different approach to the nature of the document: for most Australian companies a contract represents an attempt to control the ongoing development of a specific business relationship. It usually attempts to provide for all eventualities and sets out in detail the obligations of each party to the transaction and how these obligations are to be carried out.

For many Chinese companies, a contract is more a statement of intent which reflects the situation at the time that it was drawn up. Changing circumstances, it is felt, are likely to require changed responses, so the wording of a contract is broad to allow flexibility. Moreover, the bedrock on which the contract is based is not so much law, as it is in Australia, but relationship. A strong relationship, together with the trust that this inspires, tends to be seen as more important than reliance on an external body of law. The implication of this is that there may be pressure to revisit the provisions of a contract even after it has been signed. The feelings of outrage and betrayal that western businesspeople commonly feel at such attempts are only matched by the similar feelings that their Chinese counterparts feel when westerners do not admit that changed circumstances are a cause of re-negotiation of the contract.

While this attitude is now far less common in the coastal cities with a history of overseas business relationships, it has certainly not disappeared, and it remains an expectation in areas which have had less exposure to foreign ways of doing business. In negotiating contracts, therefore, it is useful to build in a number of provisions which can serve as bargaining chips if re-negotiation becomes necessary.

> Many Australians who have been involved in negotiating contracts in China comment that perhaps their most difficult task is negotiating with head office back home. In the light of the discussion of negotiations and contracts, why do you think this might be so?

Organisation of information

In Chapter 6, page 85, we discussed differences in the way information is organised in presenting an argument. In summary, we can say that English favours deductive argument, in which a position is presented and then followed by arguments supporting that position, while Chinese favours inductive argument, in which information is presented in such a way as to lead speaker and listener together to a particular conclusion. See also Chapter 9, page 155.

These differences help explain two common complaints. The first is the Australian one that a large amount of time in negotiations is taken up in the presentation of irrelevant detail. This complaint is largely the result of a lack of understanding of the features of inductive argument, which requires the presentation of a large amount of information to create a detailed context for the conclusion. Important points are included as part of this mass of information, and Chinese will expect that these points have been noted by the Australian side. All too often, however, Australians tune out of inductive presentations, thinking that the detail is unimportant or irrelevant. This is especially so as they do not understand where the argument is leading, as inductive argument delays the conclusion to the end. They may therefore miss important messages.

The Chinese, in contrast, are likely to pay great attention to every detail of an Australian presentation, often taking copious notes. They are likely to attach great importance to any discrepancies that they find, and even to attribute intention to these discrepancies, because they treat each presentation as inductive and each discrepancy as undermining the conclusion that is finally reached.

Faced with inductively organised presentations, Australians need to take a leaf out of the Chinese book by paying close attention to the information being presented. This may mean taking extensive notes and crosschecking information presented by each different speaker. For this reason alone it helps to have a team, so that different members can be assigned to monitor different sections of a presentation. In making presentations, they need to coordinate as closely as possible in order to avoid minor factual or other discrepancies. Above all, they need to curb feelings of impatience, to maintain an appearance of calm and to remain polite.

The second complaint is the Chinese one: that Australians (and other English speakers) are intent on forcing acceptance of their own conclusions, and are uninterested in anything that the Chinese might think. This complaint is a reaction to the upfront nature of the deductive style of argument. Being presented with a conclusion or position without, in the first instance, any information to justify that conclusion can appear uncooperative or even threatening to those more used to inductive argument.

In order to counter this impression, Australians need to demonstrate that they are in fact open to discussion. Ways of doing this include the use of informal discussions both before and during the formal negotiation process. Banquets and trips to tourist sites provide opportunities for such informal interaction, which is an important way of building relationship. The stronger the relationship, the less likely are differences in style of argument to create problems. Be ready also to repeat explanations and to provide a wide range of information in both written and visual form, more information than would be normal in negotiations within the Australian context.

Differences in the organisation of information occur not only in the course of negotiations and other spoken interactions, but also in written form in reports and other documents. This is discussed with relation to academic writing in the Chapter 9; here it is sufficient to point out that reports written by Chinese speakers may appear to

English speakers to waffle and to have difficulty getting to the point. On the other hand, many Chinese complain about the repetitive nature of English writing, which involves presenting a conclusion in the introduction, justifying the conclusion in the body and confirming the conclusion at the end. Once the reader understands the organisational strategy being employed, he or she will (hopefully) be able to adjust the way in which they read the text.

> Read a report written by a native English speaker and another translated from Chinese.
>
> a. How is the information organised in each?
>
> b. Which do you find easiest to read?
>
> Consider an inconclusive or difficult business meeting that you have attended with your Chinese counterparts.
>
> a. To what extent might differences in the way that information was presented have contributed to the difficulties experienced?

Attitude to foreigners

Chapter 7 briefly outlined some common attitudes towards foreigners. In discussing these attitudes within the business context it should be pointed out that few foreigners encounter open negative sentiment, and that the type of hostility that even recent Chinese immigrants to Australia have had in some cases to face has very seldom occurred in China.

Having said this, it is true that some sections of the population believe that foreign companies are in China only to exploit its resources and to profit from its cheap labour. Older cadres in state-owned companies are particularly likely to feel this, but the sentiment is shared by others and has crystallised to a certain extent around opposition to WTO membership. This opposition is officially discouraged and its extent is consequently difficult to gauge. While it is not likely to cause any major problems in the foreseeable future, it is a sentiment that can come to the fore as a result of other difficulties. In this it is similar to the anti-immigrant and anti-Asian feelings expressed by the likes of Pauline Hanson, which has emerged in the context of declining prosperity and loss of services in country towns and the loss of manufacturing jobs that previously offered employment to people with lower levels of education.

A related attitude is that western countries in general and western companies in particular owe a debt to China because of the long years of colonial exploitation. This attitude is felt especially strongly towards Japan, but it can also be directed at others. In order to repay this debt, some expect that companies engaged in business have a responsibility to hand over advanced technologies or to wear losses without complaint. This often goes together with a lack of understanding of the imperatives of western business, especially the emphasis on the bottom line, and a belief that western companies are all rich. These beliefs are not as outlandish as they may appear to western businesspeople, in that for most of the last 50 years, the aims of state-owned enterprises have been social rather than commercial.

Finally, the desire to modernise as quickly as possible may lead to a demand for the latest technology and a reluctance to use older technologies even if these are more appropriate for local conditions. Some may believe that attempts to use less than cutting-edge technology represents a deliberate attempt to hold back China's modernisation process.

It is not suggested that anti-foreign feeling is likely to be a major problem, but it is important to recognise that these latent attitudes can emerge in the context of an already difficult relationship. It is also important to acknowledge the ease with which anti-Chinese attitudes can develop among Australian businesspeople as a result of differences in basic understandings and attitudes. In fact, the emergence of an 'us and them' attitude, as in 'they' do this and 'they' do that, should serve as a warning bell. Once it is noticed, it is useful to attempt to understand things from the Chinese point of view, using an understanding of Chinese attitudes and values as a guide. Most important is the need to remember that logic and right are shared commodities, not the exclusive possession of one or the other.

Working with interpreters

If you do not speak Chinese and you are involved in business in China, you are inevitably going to need a good interpreter. This is something that requires careful attention, and should not be left to the last minute. The first thing to consider is the role that the interpreter is expected to play. She may restrict herself to presenting as accurately as possible the words that are spoken by each side in an interaction. She may, however, go further and she may explain features of the context, commenting on things left unsaid, or on body language, or explain aspects of Chinese business practice. She may advise you on the most effective ways of getting a message across. In other words, a good interpreter can play a vital role in establishing and maintaining clear, polite and effective communication with Chinese counterparts.

Another consideration is that of technical language. If the content of discussions is technical, it is important to use an interpreter who is familiar with the concepts involved and can translate them accurately. One of the best Chinese films of the 1980s, *The black cannon incident*, deals in part with the havoc caused when a general translator is used to translate specialist engineering terminology. Some companies deal with this problem by delegating a bilingual member of the technical team to translate, effectively giving them two jobs. This may not be an efficient option, because the person concerned may not be able to give their full attention to either responsibility.

Two things are implied by these points. The first is that interpreters are highly skilled professionals whose work needs to be taken seriously. The second is that it is usually preferable to employ an interpreter rather than rely on Chinese partners to provide one, or, even worse, to expect a single interpreter to translate for both sides. This may impose an enormous burden and greatly magnify the risk of miscommunication, especially as an interpreter who is on the payroll will have the interests of the company at heart. The team will also be able to avail itself of the understanding of the Chinese business environment that a good interpreter should have.

Working effectively with an interpreter is an art. Firstly, it is important to fully brief the interpreter regarding the issues under discussion and the positions that the team will be putting. If the discussion is likely to focus on technical issues, it is worth assembling a glossary of the terms that are likely to come up and to go through it together beforehand. If a formal speech is to be translated, try to give the interpreter a copy in advance. These steps will assist in getting points across clearly and concisely.

Secondly, when using a translator remember to pause after each three to four sentences, trying to time the pauses so that they occur at natural breaks or changes in the subject matter. Keep language simple and relatively formal: the more informal the language, the greater the difficulty the interpreter is likely to face in translating it. Avoid the use of slang and colloquialisms, which may be unfamiliar to the interpreter. A lovely story about the use of one typically Australian colloquialism is told about Bob Hawke's visit to China in the mid-1980s. The story goes that Hawke was making an important speech in the presence of several of China's most senior leaders when he assured them that Australia was not playing silly buggers regarding a particular issue. The interpreter, in full flight, got as far as 'silly' before skidding to a shuddering halt, while the official members of the Australian delegation proved their sterling worth by remaining poker-faced, albeit at great cost.

Remember to address all remarks to your Chinese counterparts and remain looking at them while the interpreter is translating: this will allow you to monitor how your comments are being received.

Use visual aids as much as possible to illustrate the points that you are making. Charts, graphs, diagrams and photographs can greatly increase the force of a presentation.

Finally, remember that your interpreter is human: be aware of how fatigue, stress, hunger and even alcohol might affect the quality of translation, especially at the end of a long day. Make sure that breaks are built into the schedule.

Notes

1 Blackman, C. (2000). *China business: The rules of the game*. Sydney: Allen & Unwin, pp 95–99.

2 Orton, J. (2000). *Keys to successful intercultural communication in Australian-Chinese joint ventures*. The Australia China Business Council (Vic. Branch).

3 Thousand year eggs are not, obviously, one thousand years old, but have been subject to a preservative process which turns the yolk a dark blue black and the white a dark clear colour varying from brown to black. In Chinese they are *song hua dan*, 'pine flower eggs', because of the fine mottling that they display. They have an unusual and delicate taste which is worth getting used to, unlikely as that may seem.

4 If you are entertaining at a Chinese restaurant in Australia, make sure that you specify that your guests will be Chinese. This is because it is very difficult for non-Chinese Australians to get authentic Chinese meals. Mostly they are served modified versions of dishes in the mistaken belief that non-Chinese don't like authentic Chinese food.

CHAPTER NINE

LEARNING AND TEACHING

The classroom is in itself a cross-cultural laboratory. When entering the classroom, Chinese learners bring with them a whole series of assumptions based on their previous experience as learners. These assumptions are both conscious and unconscious and include ideas about the nature and purpose of learning in general and language learning in particular, ideas about the role of the learner and the role of the teacher, about effective and ineffective study methods, about the nature of syllabus and about the usefulness or otherwise of a wide range of teaching and learning techniques. At the same time, western-educated teachers may bring a completely different set of assumptions, many of which conflict with those of their students. In this chapter, we will explore some of these assumptions.

> The trouble with Chinese teachers is that they've never done any real teacher-training courses so they don't know how to teach. All they do is follow the book. They never give us any opportunity to talk. How in the world do they expect us to learn?
>
> Australian student, Shanghai, 1988
>
> Australian teachers are very friendly but they often can't teach very well. I never know where they're going – there's no system and I just get lost. Also, they're often badly trained and don't really have a thorough grasp of their subject.
>
> Chinese student, Sydney, 1990
>
> From your own experience and from what you have already read, how would you explain these two comments?

What is learning? What is teaching?

The Chinese attitude to learning and teaching has something in common with traditional western attitudes. For both, learning involves mastering a body of knowledge, a body of knowledge that is presented by a teacher in hunks small enough to be relatively easily digested. Both teachers and learners are concerned with the end product of learning – that is, they expect that the learner will, at an appropriate time, be able to reproduce the knowledge in the same form as it was presented by the teacher.

Such an attitude to Chinese learning and teaching appears to pay little attention to self-expression, the encouragement of which is generally believed to be one of the key aims of western education. Most Chinese teachers would answer this by analogy. In order to perform a concerto, you first need to be able to play an instrument; that is, you must at least have mastered certain physical abilities. So it is in other fields. Learners must first master the basics and only when this is accomplished are they in a position to use what they have mastered in a creative manner.

If learning involves the mastery of a body of knowledge, then teaching involves the presentation of this body in such a way that it can be mastered relatively painlessly. To facilitate mastery, knowledge is usually regarded as inherently divisible into small blocks, one of which leads on to the next. So A leads on to B which in turn leads on to C.

Learning a language therefore becomes rather like climbing a ladder. As long as the first rung is firm, the learner can easily climb to the second rung, and so on. In the case of language, the rungs of the ladder are composed of grammar and vocabulary. If both are arranged in ascending order of difficulty and presented in blocks of manageable size, with clear explanations, then the probability of successful learning is high.

Because learning is essentially seen as the mastery of a body of knowledge, deductive presentation tends to be favoured over inductive, and the teaching and use of learning strategies such as prediction and contextualisation are in general neglected. A further result is that, in language teaching, the use of the mother tongue tends to be stressed, especially at the lower levels. Using the mother tongue helps the teacher present knowledge of the new language in an easily assimilable way.

> You mean ... you want me to guess?
>> Chinese teacher of English, on being faced with an exercise
>> dealing with the use of contextual clues
>
> Why might this teacher object to 'guessing' as a learning strategy?

> Imagine that you are a Chinese teacher of English.
>
> Explain to an Australian colleague why you use Chinese with your lower level classes and why you encourage learners to use a bilingual dictionary.
>
> Then ask your Chinese students about the benefits of using Chinese and a bilingual dictionary. Do your reasons agree with theirs? Why or why not?

What is the role of the teacher?

If learning involves the mastery of a body of knowledge, then teachers are people who have already mastered that body of knowledge and are prepared to hand it on to learners. Teachers are therefore both givers and knowers.

As givers, teachers are responsible for arranging and presenting knowledge in the most accessible way possible. This firstly involves selecting the material to be taught. Material is usually selected by reference to the total body of knowledge available and to the degree of difficulty involved.

This contrasts with the concept of learner need which is widely used by syllabus designers and teachers in English speaking countries when deciding what to teach. Chinese teachers and textbook writers tend to refer to the body of English texts and grammar and from this choose what they consider to be basic: the grammatical rules that can most readily be built on, the vocabulary that has the widest currency.

Many Chinese learners are surprised to be asked by their Australian teachers what they want to learn. They tend to feel that they lack the knowledge to make an informed decision and moreover believe that is one of a teacher's most basic duties. Having chosen the material to be taught, the teacher's next responsibility is to ensure that it is divided logically into a series of steps, starting with the most basic and moving on from there. Within the Chinese education system, at both secondary and tertiary levels, these twin responsibilities are usually shared between the teacher and the textbook writer. However, while teachers are usually constrained by the textbook, they remain responsible for presenting textbook material in digestible form.

The teachers' main responsibility, however, and the one by which they are usually judged, is their ability to explain the selected material. Clear presentation and explanation of each step in the learning chain are seen as keys to ease of learning. And learning essentially means knowing and understanding.

With the stress being laid on knowing and understanding, there tends to be resistance to such common Australian (and western) teaching techniques as finding the main idea or using context to interpret unknown words. The first involves leaving some aspects of the text unexplained, unknown and unlearned. The second relies on guessing rather than knowing. Both violate the teacher's fundamental responsibility.

Another consequence of this view of a teacher's responsibilities is that a teacher is responsible to a very high degree for a learner's progress. If students are not progressing in a satisfactory manner, they may feel that the teacher has failed to present and explain material clearly enough.

As well as being givers, teachers are also knowers. This means that they are expected to have a detailed knowledge of their subject and to be able to answer questions raised by learners on any aspect of it. Mastery of subject matter is, in fact, considered fundamental to being a good teacher. Teachers who are unable to answer a question and admit as much run a grave risk of being considered lazy, incompetent or both.

If a teacher makes a mistake, this also tends to be regarded seriously. A learner noticing such a mistake would often not point it out publicly, but would rather approach the teacher privately after class. Again, the learner would usually avoid directly commenting on the error, but would refer to an impartial source such as a textbook. Typically, the learner would ask the teacher to explain the apparent contradiction between what the book says and what the teacher has said.

Chinese teachers tend to have a rather wider pastoral role than most western teachers would expect. They are expected to set an example, especially in relation to standards of conduct. Many are consulted by their students regarding possible future courses of action, and especially future courses of study. Parents and teachers have great influence over decisions.

Some Chinese students may interpret the relatively egalitarian approach of their Australian teachers as signalling a willingness to help them outside class time, and may consequently feel misled when they find that this is not usually so.

Finally, many Chinese learners find it difficult to take seriously teachers whose dress is not neat and tidy. Untidy, unusual or dirty clothes are often taken to mean that the person in question is not well educated, and so is obviously unfit to be a teacher. This is especially true for female teachers, though male teachers may be judged in a like manner. One British male teacher teaching in a Chinese university came to class one day with a piece of plastic cord in place of a shoelace in one shoe. The next day he found several pairs of shoelaces, all of the appropriate colour, arranged neatly on his desk.

There is a Chinese tradition that people, or more accurately, men of great wisdom have not time for such mundane trifles as neat clothing. However, any foreign male teacher seeking to benefit from this belief should ensure that his teaching does in fact embody the wisdom that he claims via the manner of his dress.

What do you consider a teacher's role to be?

How does your concept of the role differ from that described above?

What difficulties do you think you might have teaching in the Chinese system?

What difficulties might Chinese students face in adapting to your understanding of a teacher's role?

How might you help them adapt?

What is the role of the student?

As teachers are givers, so students are receivers. Their job is to master the knowledge that the teacher presents. A good student tends to be one who can most accurately recall the knowledge presented. Students are not expected to argue with the teacher or to present their own ideas, at least until they have mastered sufficient of the body of knowledge to be able to make informed judgments. This does not mean that students do not have any opinions. However, many may feel that the classroom, and particularly the language classroom, is not the place to air them. Language learning is, after all, about learning a language rather than presenting opinions! Most students are more than willing to participate once they see the relation between such participation and language learning; that is, once they understand the reasoning behind the teacher's demands.

Good students know the answers to their teachers' questions. Many students may be reluctant to volunteer answers to questions unless they are sure they are correct. 'Guessing' the answer is not encouraged because it shows that the student in question has not mastered the material and explanations presented.

In general, volunteering answers to questions is also discouraged by a fear of being seen as too pushy. This is especially true of women, some of whom fear losing their femininity by being too aggressive. Nominating particular students to give answers is, however, common and most Chinese students will give an answer if nominated even though they would hesitate to volunteer one.

The expectation remains, however, that the answer will be the correct one because the student has previewed the lesson under consideration and reviewed the previous one. Some students may feel unfairly 'put on the spot' when, in Australia, they are asked to answer questions they have had little or no time to prepare for.

The preview and review of lessons constitute a fundamental student responsibility. Preview of the material for the next lesson allows the student not only to prepare correct answers to the teacher's questions but also to identify problem areas. Review allows the material to be memorised while the teacher's explanations are still fresh in mind, and it prepares the ground on which the next lesson will be built.

From the students' point of view, the main sources of knowledge available are the teacher and the textbook. The textbook lays out the knowledge to be mastered and the teacher's role is to elucidate that material. Sources of knowledge outside the classroom, including the library, television and other media, and personal contact with native speakers, tend to be given a lesser importance because there is no teacher available to explain. Thus, while students will tend to expect that television and newspapers might be used in Australian classrooms, they may ignore such resources outside the classroom. This, of course, has important implications for self-directed learning.

A good student being one who masters the knowledge presented to him, naturally implies that this knowledge will be specifically tested. Most Chinese students expect to have regular tests and examinations to help them measure how much of the presented material has been memorised. They further expect that tests will focus on material presented in class, and they may resent tests that measure language proficiency, as there is no obvious method of studying for such examinations.

What do you consider to be the characteristics of a good student?

How does your list of characteristics compare with the Chinese list outlined above?

Before reading the following section, quickly jot down what you think Chinese students might feel about the common teaching and learning strategies and techniques listed below. Base your answers on your own experiences and on what you have already read.

a. peer correction

b. learning songs

c. self-assessment

d. excursions

e. vocabulary lists

f. grammar exercises

g. theme-based teaching

h. textbooks

i. bilingual dictionaries

j. role-play.

Student expectations in the classroom

Given the stress on learning as mastery of a body of knowledge, it is not surprising that most Chinese students express a strong preference for courses based on textbooks. The textbook sets out the body of knowledge to be learned and allows the student to work through it in an orderly and progressive fashion. It allows for specific testing, so that the student has an objective guide to progress (or lack of it!); it allows for preview and review and in general provides a route map to guide the learning process. In practice, in Chinese classrooms little distinction is made between the textbook and the syllabus, the textbook in fact becoming the syllabus.

Without this 'route map', Chinese learners may feel acutely disorientated. They may feel that there is no system to what they are learning and no attempt to build from one grammatical point to the next or from one lesson to the next. Common themes, such as 'Getting a job' or 'Pollution', tend to be seen as a useful way of organising new vocabulary, but not as a substitute for the systematic presentation of the grammar of a language. However, over the last decade, Chinese textbooks have paid greater attention to the purpose to which a language is put, so Chinese students are likely to be more familiar with current western approaches to language teaching than was previously the case.

In spite of this, without a textbook students tend to find it difficult to preview lessons and many complain that as a result they are unprepared for the new material that the teacher presents to them. It also means that they feel they have insufficient opportunity either to find the correct answer to possible questions or to sort out what they do not understand from what they do understand.

The issue of 'the correct answer' is important. Questions are usually regarded as having right and wrong answers, with no room for uncertainty or for trial and error. Many students prefer to avoid situations where they run the risk of giving a wrong answer for reasons explained above. They may therefore be reluctant to volunteer answers. A student who, when nominated, is unable to answer a question may prefer silence to the admission of ignorance. Many prefer to read the answer to a question from the relevant section of the text rather than putting the information in their own words. This indicates that they understand the question and know the answer while at the same time are hopefully avoiding grammatical errors.

Most students tend to look to the teacher and the textbook as providers of the correct answer. Fellow students are usually regarded by definition as unsuitable. Few are likely to see much value in peer correction and many regard it as a waste of time at best and a symptom of the teacher's lack of preparation at worst.

Since language learning is concerned with knowing the grammar and vocabulary of a language, most students feel that grammar and vocabulary should form the core of any course, and many feel that a lesson in which they have spent an hour in discussion but have not in the end got a list of new words or grammar points to review has been a waste of time.

This does not mean that Chinese students are reluctant to take part in discussions, role-plays and dialogues, but that they may prefer such activities to be closely linked to the practice of new vocabulary or specific grammatical points.

Attitudes to classroom activities tend also to be influenced by the attitude that learning is a serious business. For many Australian teachers, learning is an activity that is made more palatable, and probably even more effective, if it is enjoyable. This attitude is so pervasive that a common answer to the perennial teacher's question 'How did it go?' is 'Oh, it went very well. They really enjoyed it'. The equation of enjoyment and learning is not an equation commonly made by Chinese students. Some may even feel that enjoyment is detrimental to learning. At best, enjoyment is likely to be seen as an optional extra rather than a necessity. This attitude is especially relevant in relation to activities such as the teaching of songs. Many teachers have been puzzled by what appears to be enthusiastic participation coupled with later comments that nothing was being learned! Again, this does not mean that songs, for example, have no place in the language classroom, but that Australian teachers need to be aware of the criteria for judging the success of a lesson.

The idea of self-assessment is one that many Chinese students regard with suspicion. Many students believe assessment is the responsibility of the teacher, as it involves measuring where the student is as against where they should be, given the time spent. Only the teacher has the requisite knowledge to perform such a judgment. Attempts to get students to self-assess may therefore be regarded at best as a waste of time and at worst as proof of abdication of teacher responsibility.

Tests and examinations are a regular and expected feature of Chinese education. They are also accepted as legitimate tests of progress and ability Their aim is, however, to check that students have mastered the requisite body of knowledge, and many consist mainly or entirely of multiple choice questions. Marks therefore tend to be high by Australian standards, with the pass mark being set at 60 per cent and the majority of students scoring in the 80s and 90s. Chinese students in Australia may be shocked and discouraged when they encounter the Australian marking system for the first time.

Information order in essays

In Chapter 6, page 85, we discussed differences between English and Chinese in the ways in which information is organised in an argument. These differences are especially important when Chinese students undertake tertiary study in English-medium universities in Australia or elsewhere because of the requirements of essay and report writing.

Here is a short essay written by a Chinese student in response to the question *Discuss the implications for copyright of the Napster case.*

1 In the last few months, the Napster case has raised many issues related to copyright. Napster is a United States company created in August 1999 by a 19-year-old boy called Shawn Fanning. He wrote a piece of software in his dorm room on Hemingway Street. It allowed users to share and download music files. This software now has more than 57 million registered users, with 1.6 million exchanging digital music at any time. Napster has many features which allow users to do such things as search for MP3 files, play MP3 files, and chat with other MP3 users.

2 The RIAA (Recording Industry Association of America), which represents the major record labels, claims that many Internet users have downloaded Napster's

software and are sharing millions of files of copyrighted music using the MP3 format. It is suing Napster for contributing to copyright violations and explicit copyright infringement. In its brief, the association quote a survey it commissioned by the Field Research Corp that stated 22 per cent of Napster users said that because of Napster they did not buy CDs any more, or bought fewer CDs. It wants to shut down Napster for good in order to fix the problem.

3 Napster is saying that Napster's users are doing nothing wrong by making personal collections of music they download from the Internet.

> If a consumer can copy an MP3 file from his or her hard drive without violating the copyright laws, it is self-evident that Napster's Internet directory service does not violate the copyright laws either, according to the brief. In turn, if individual users are not guilty of copyright infringement then the company cannot be guilty of contributory infringement, Mr Boise said in an interview.
>
> The New York Times

4 In order to avoid charges of encouraging copyright infringement, Napster has blocked one million songs, but Napster cannot check its users' files to see if there has been a copyright violation. And Napster is planning to create a subscription version that would charge customers a fee. The company has already made a deal with Bertelsmann, the parent company of BMG Entertainment. They are going forward with the proposed fee-based system, which they say will be in place by summer. The model includes a basic membership plan for users. Thomas Middelhoff, the chief executive of Bertelsmann, said that he was confident that many users of the Napster software would be happy to pay for music. A survey carried out recently showed that 80 per cent of Napster's users would be willing to pay about $15 a month for the subscription fee.

5 Napster is good software which allows users to access the users' databases for MP3 files and download them. But Napster must realise that it doesn't have a license to allow trading files between users. So, Napster should charge for its MP3 file-sharing system, and get a license from the recording company and make everything legal.

English teachers typically comment on the organisation of this essay in terms such as:

- lacks a clear introduction and thesis statement presenting the main argument of the essay
- includes too much irrelevant and incidental detail
- lacks coherent argument
- conclusion not supported by evidence presented in body of essay.

They expect an essay to display a deductive organisation involving three major stages:

- an introduction which most importantly indicates the argument to be presented

- a body which outlines a series of points supporting the argument and/or dismissing points against it

- a conclusion which summarises the argument and supports, modifies or rarely dismisses the position stated in the introduction.

As the teachers' comments reveal, the Napster essay is not organised deductively, rather it utilises an inductive form of argument. Inductive argument involves presenting a range of information to the reader in such a way as to guide reader and writer together to a conclusion. Let us examine how this form of organisation is represented in the Napster essay.

Paragraph 1 sets the Napster issue in a context by explaining how the software came to be developed. It then outlines what the program does and how it is used. Paragraph 2 presents the copyright issue raised by Napster and summarises the RIAA case against the software. Paragraphs 3 and 4 outline Napster's defence against the RIAA accusations and the steps that the software developers have taken to avoid any future copyright violations. Finally, paragraph 5 presents the writer's conclusion by endorsing the RIAA claim that unauthorised trading is unacceptable and by pointing to Napster's actions to overcome the problem.

In this case, discussion with the writer of the essay made it quite clear that he felt confident that his argument was clearly and logically organised. He was confused by his teacher's criticisms regarding lack of focus and in fact decided that the teacher was discriminating against him on racial grounds. His teacher was equally puzzled by the student's lack of understanding of the requirements of essay organisation and concluded that he just did not listen in class.

The point being made here is not that English organises information deductively while Chinese organises it inductively. Both languages have the capacity to use each form of organisation. However, there is a strong tendency for English to privilege deductive organisation and for Chinese to privilege inductive organisation. So marked is this preference that most English speakers fail to recognise examples of inductive organisation, and experience such organisation as confused and meaningless, while many Chinese speakers regard deductive organisation as unnecessary and meaningless repetition.

When teaching Chinese students essay organisation, it is often not enough to merely outline the standard stages of a deductively organised essay. Such an approach may result only in the incorporation of a thesis statement into the first paragraph of an otherwise inductively organised essay. This is because many students may feel that they already know how to write an essay and so miss the significance of the points that their English teachers are making. Teachers need to assist students to analyse examples of both inductive and deductive argument and to identify the characteristic features of each. Once this is done, students are in a better position to appreciate the demands of essay writing in an English-language tertiary environment.

Teachers also need to comment on their students' essays in the light of an understanding of the differences between the two approaches. This means that rather than highlighting the deficiencies of an essay from a deductive point of view, they might find it more effective to acknowledge an essay's inductive features before indicating how these need to be recast in a deductive essay.

Using information: The issue of plagiarism

In recent years considerable attention has been directed towards what has been seen as an increasing incidence of plagiarism among tertiary students. The issue of plagiarism raises special problems for many overseas students, and for Chinese students in particular, because of differences in understandings relating to knowledge and to the role of the student in the learning process.

The approach to knowledge embodied in current Chinese learning and teaching practice tends to stress knowledge as unproblematic; that is, as a collection of theories, concepts and facts that are broadly speaking not contested. Knowledge advances through accretion – that is, by adding to and developing currently existing knowledge. Little attention is given, in the social sciences and the humanities in particular, to the possibility of alternative approaches to problems. (This does not imply that Chinese scholarship is uncritical; merely that students tend not to be expected to be critical at the secondary and early tertiary levels.) It is the student's task to acquire the unitary body of knowledge that constitutes the subject being studied, and to reproduce it on demand, in examinations for example, or in essays. It is not the student's role to adjudicate between conflicting positions or to develop a position of his or her own. This comes later, after a body of knowledge sufficiently extensive to support critical analysis has been acquired. Students are not therefore expected to develop an individual voice: their voice is the voice of the literature of the discipline they are studying.

Before we draw out the implications of this position for both essay writing and for plagiarism, it might be useful to briefly explore some of the assumptions that underlie much of western practice in learning and teaching. Knowledge within this tradition tends to be regarded as developed through competition between ideas. It is therefore seen as partial and problematic. The student's role within this system tends to be that of participant, albeit at a junior level, in an on-going discussion. He or she is expected to evaluate various positions and to develop an individual voice which presents a particular position and defends this position against others. This requires that the student's voice be distinguished from other voices in the discussion, and that other voices be distinguished from each other.

The implications of these two general positions for essay and report writing are profound. The western teacher tends to expect a carefully argued position in which the student's voice is clear and in which other voices are clearly identified and either critiqued or used to support the student's position. The Chinese teacher is more likely to expect a presentation of the body of knowledge relevant to the topic. Much less stress is likely to be placed either on the expression of a clear student voice or on distinguishing the various voices in the literature. In fact, many Chinese students express amazement when asked to present a position of their own, as they feel that they do not have either the knowledge or the experience to do so.

With specific regard to plagiarism, many Chinese students do not feel any great need to meticulously cite all their sources as they feel their task is to master a body of knowledge; that is, to merge their voice with that of the literature.

Unfortunately, many Australian academics tend to regard plagiarism as a moral issue, as akin to theft if not as theft itself. Their response is often punitive, as is witnessed by the statements on plagiarism that are printed in the opening pages of almost all university handbooks and handed out together with essay topics at the beginning of each term. Large sections of such statements are taken up with a description of the penalties incurred by plagiarists. Such exhortations regularly fall on deaf ears primarily because, without a change in understanding of the role of a student in relationship to learning and knowledge, plagiarism remains an abstract and obscure concept. In order to actually reduce the incidence of plagiarism, teachers, and especially English teachers, will need to make western assumptions regarding student roles much more transparent. Furthermore, they need to set this discussion within a cultural framework that allows Chinese students to identify similarities and differences between western and Chinese concepts of how knowledge is developed and the role of a student in relationship to that knowledge.

Classroom Tasks

■ TASK 1 ■

What is plagiarism?

Write a brief definition in the space below.

■ TASK 2 ■

You have been asked to write an essay on the difficulties that foreign students face in studying in Australia. You wish to use information presented in Tomoko Koyama's book *Japan: A handbook in intercultural communication* (published by NCELTR in 1992) in order to support a point that you are making.

Below you will find several different ways of using the information. Decide which are acceptable and which would be considered plagiarism. Give your reasons.

Original text

An interesting feature of Japanese housing is that many houses have a guest room which is used for receiving and entertaining guests. Unlike the Australian family, which gives its guests a tour of the house, Japanese expect their guests to remain in the guest room. They therefore often experience culture shock when invited to Australian homes. One Japanese couple reported that they had been invited to an Australian party and were surprised to see all the female guests gathered in the kitchen chatting with the hostess.

Version	Evaluation
1. Japanese students in Australia may face problems because of differences in attitudes to public and private space. An interesting feature of Japanese housing is that many houses have a guest room which is used for receiving and entertaining guests. One Japanese couple reported that they had been invited to an Australian party and were surprised to see all the female guests gathered in the kitchen chatting with the hostess. For Japanese, the kitchen is private space, while most Australians would regard it a public space and therefore open to guests.	
2. Japanese students in Australia may face problems because of differences in attitudes to public and private space. Koyama (1992) reports on a Japanese couple who had been invited to an Australian party and were surprised to see all the female guests gathered in the kitchen chatting with the hostess. Most Japanese would regard the kitchen as private space, and therefore not an appropriate place for guests to gather.	
3. Japanese students in Australia may face problems because of differences in attitudes to public and private space. A Japanese couple said that they went to an Australian party and all the guests gathered in the kitchen chatting with the hostess. Most Japanese would regard the kitchen as private space, and therefore not an appropriate place for guests to gather.	
4. Japanese students in Australia may face problems because of differences in attitudes to public and private space. Koyama (1992) explains that many Japanese houses have a guest room and guests are not expected to enter other rooms. She quotes the shock one couple expressed at finding the female guests at a party talking to their hostess in the kitchen. Most Japanese would regard the kitchen as private space, and therefore not an appropriate place for guests to gather.	

The teaching of English in China

English-language teaching in Chinese universities usually focuses on five major areas: intensive reading, extensive reading, grammar, listening and oral English. Writing is usually not introduced until late, often not until the third year of a four-year course. Of the five major areas, intensive reading, grammar and listening tend to be most important. Intensive reading, as its name suggests, involves the careful study of a text, so that each item of vocabulary is understood and every grammatical feature is explained. Associated exercises usually include detailed comprehension questions, vocabulary matching and sentence rewriting. Students may also be expected to write summaries of the text.

Grammar lessons attempt to build a logical knowledge of the language, with each step building on the previous one. The grammatical structures to be taught are usually introduced in a text, the features of which are then explained in Chinese. Common exercise types include sentence transformations (such as active to passive, present to past), various types of sentence completion (putting the word in brackets in the correct tense, for example), cloze exercises, translations from Chinese to English and from English to Chinese and punctuation exercises.

Listening texts include dialogues, stories, short lectures and news items. General comprehension questions are asked and students are often required to summarise the contents of the story or to repeat the dialogue.

Oral English lessons make use of similar exercise types, students often being required to listen to dialogues and repeat them before producing their own version based on a related situation. Retelling the story is also a popular exercise type.

Finally, extensive reading involves students with longer works in English, often works of 19th century literature. Lessons here focus on the historical and cultural background to the work in question. Students are expected to follow the story but there is no attempt to have them understand every word.

In all language teaching, modelling plays an important role, with the teacher providing an appropriate sample dialogue or written text and the students using this as a basis to be modified along lines that are also specified by the teacher.

Many of the assumptions that a Chinese student brings into the Australian classroom are naturally based on his or her previous language learning experience. The student is likely to feel disorientated when confronted with a teaching method that stresses use of the language rather than knowledge about the language, which treats the teacher as a facilitator of learning rather than a fount of knowledge, and which downplays notions of language as a grammatical system in favour of language as a means of achieving an end. Suddenly they are themselves the determiners of what is or is not useful, they are expected to enjoy learning, to make mistakes, to take risks and above all to focus on the process of learning rather than the product. While helping their students to adapt to this new way of learning, teachers might profitably remember that the Chinese system has produced countless competent speakers of English and that in many cases their students' grasp of English is better than their own grasp of Chinese or any other tongue.

The Chinese education system

Chinese education is, in theory, free, universal and compulsory, and every child is required to complete nine years of primary and middle school education. In the cities this is in fact achieved, but the record is less successful in the countryside.

Secondary education is divided into two stages, called junior and senior middle school respectively. Examinations at the end of the third year of junior middle school determine if a student will continue into the senior school, enrol in a vocational training school or leave school altogether. Vocational schools prepare students for a wide range of skilled and semi-skilled jobs. Students who continue into senior high school engage in preparation for the gruelling examinations that control entry into tertiary education.

Choice of subjects is limited at all levels. At the senior level students elect to study in one of two broad areas: the sciences, or the social sciences and arts. English is compulsory in both streams. Classes are large, averaging 40 to 50 students, and facilities, including library facilities, are limited. Students are expected to study very hard, and those hoping to get into university do in fact put in long hours. Classes are held six days a week starting at about eight in the morning and finishing about five in the evening, including a rest period of about one and a half hours at lunchtime.

Entry to university is extremely competitive and only a small percentage of applicants are accepted. However, since the mid-1990s the government has made a concerted effort to expand the number of places available, with the result that in the early years of the third millennium about 15 per cent of young people were involved in some form of tertiary education. One of the results of this move has been that many universities now offer special courses to those who have failed to gain admission through the examination system. In some cases, such courses are developed in partnership with a foreign university. Students undertaking such courses usually study separately from those undertaking normal courses and are often looked down on as being less capable and less motivated.

All students pay tuition fees, which in 2003 amounted to approximately 70 per cent of an average annual household income for city dwellers, and double the average annual income of an agricultural family.

Students apply to enrol in a specific course and once accepted in that course have little choice in the subjects they study. (The situation is similar to that of an Australian student choosing to study medicine, where most of the courses are compulsory and are studied by all medical students.) In addition to studies in their major fields of interest, all students study politics, and physical education is usually compulsory. Most courses, regardless of subject, also require one semester of English. However, as various classes are often amalgamated for the English section of the course, resulting in up to 200 students studying together, and as the time involved is usually only two to four hours a week, the results are not startling.

Students studying a course form a class and usually study and live together for the four years that constitute the average degree course. Their days are tightly programmed, and formal classes occupy most of the day. Attendance at class is compulsory and, as the main sources of information are lectures and the set text, students do in fact attend.

Libraries tend to be poorly stocked, which increases student dependence on the teacher and the text.

While some essay writing is expected, most student assessment is by way of multiple-choice examinations which are held at the end of each semester.

Most university students live on campus, even if they are studying in their own home town. They are accommodated in dormitories, the average dormitory in a good university accommodating seven students. Each student has a bunk bed, a small desk and a limited amount of storage space for clothes. All meals are taken in student canteens. Daily life is regimented, students being woken by a bell at six in the morning and lights being turned out about eleven at night. Clubs and societies are limited in number and carefully controlled.

As the students live and study together in this way, it is not surprising that the ties formed at university tend to be lifelong ties. The classmate relationship has a strength and importance that has no real counterpart in Australian university life.

Imagine that you are going to study Chinese in China.

Keeping in mind the above description of Chinese teaching methods, what difficulties would you expect to encounter in undertaking your course?

How do you think you might cope with these difficulties?

How far should teachers be prepared to modify:

a. syllabus design

b. teaching techniques

in order to accommodate student expectations?

What modifications could you make to your current teaching practices in order to do so?

Classroom Tasks

■ TASK 1 ■

Divide into groups of four. On large sheets of butcher's paper, draw a typical Chinese classroom and a typical Australian classroom.

List the differences. Compare your drawings with the drawings of other groups.

In groups, fill in the following table with the advantages and disadvantages of each system of organisation.

Chinese classrooms	Australian classrooms
Advantages	Advantages
Disadvantages	Disadvantages

■ TASK 2 ■

Imagine that you have been selected to take part in a teacher exchange program and will spend one year teaching English in a Chinese university. At the same time, a Chinese teacher will spend a year teaching English in an Australian university.

a. What differences in teaching approach would you expect to encounter?

b. Which of these differences might you find hardest to cope with?

c. How might you cope with these difficulties?

d. What difficulties do you think the Chinese teacher might encounter in Australia?

e. What advice would you give to that teacher to help him or her cope?

■ TASK 3 ■

Several friends have asked you to teach them some basic Chinese, so you have decided to teach them how to give their name, their nationality and the city they come from.

Design a lesson to teach them how to say these things. Some questions to consider:

a. Will you use English in the lesson? Why or why not?

b. Which will you use most – reading, writing, listening or speaking?

c. What types of exercises will you use for practice?

d. How long will the lesson be?

When you have finished, try it on your teacher or on a friend.

■ TASK 4 ■

Look at the lesson you wrote to teach a friend some basic Chinese.

Compare your lesson with the first lesson in a textbook aimed at students who are just beginning to learn English.

What are the similarities and differences?

ANNOTATED BIBLIOGRAPHY

Cross-cultural communication

Brislin, R. W. (1981). *Cross-cultural encounters*. New York: Pergamon.
A useful introduction to the basic questions of cross-cultural training.

Gao, G., & Ting-Toomey, S. (1998). *Communicating effectively with the Chinese.* CA: Sage.

Hofstede, G. (1980). *Culture's consequences: International differences in work-related values*. CA: Sage.
One of the most influential studies of the influence of cultural differences on business and management.

Scollon, R., & Scollon, S. W. (1995). *Intercultural communication*. Oxford: Blackwell.
An extremely useful linguistic approach to the analysis of intercultural communication.

Trompenaars, F., & Hampden-Turner, C. (1997). *Riding the waves of culture: Understanding cultural diversity in business*. London: Nicholas Brealey Publishing.
An influential analysis of cultural difference in seven key dimensions of business behaviour.

Chinese history

Luo, G. (1970 c1959). *Romance of the three kingdoms*. C. H. Brewitt-Taylor (Trans.). Rutland, Vt: C. E. Tuttle.

Nathan, A. J., & Gilley, B. (Eds.). (2002). *China's new rulers: The secret files*. London: Granta Books.
Based on internal Chinese sources, this book provides insight into the Fourth Generation: the leaders who assumed power in China at the beginning of the new millennium.

Spence, J. D. (1990). *The search for modern China*. London: Century Hutchinson.
A *tour de force* through 400 years of Chinese history from the end of the Ming to the events of 1989, focusing on China's attempts to modernise, recounted through the eyes of the participants themselves.

Chinese literature

Barmé, G., & Minford, J. (Eds.). (1988). *Seeds of fire*. New York: Hill and Wang.
An excellent anthology of recent literature from the People's Republic of China. Included are the works of novelists, poets, critics, political and human rights activists and others whose works have aroused considerable controversy in China.

Cao, X. (1973–86). *The story of the stone: A Chinese novel in five volumes.* D. Hawkes & J. Minford (Trans.). Hammondsworth: Penguin.
More commonly known in English as *The dream of red mansions*, this is one of the great novels of world literature.

Doing business in China

Blackman, C. (2000). *China business: The rules of the game.* Sydney: Allen & Unwin.
A discussion of the 'rules' for doing business in China, based on a useful series of case studies.

Blackman, C. (1997). *Negotiating China: Case studies and strategies.* Sydney: Allen & Unwin.

Orton, J. (2004). Australia–China relations in business – an intercultural perspective. In N. Thomas (Ed.), *Re-orienting Australia–China relations* (pp. 110–125). London: Ashgate.

Miscellaneous

Edwards, R. R., Henkin, L., & Nathan, A. J. (1986). *Human rights in contemporary China.* New York: Columbia University Press.
An intelligent attempt to relate human rights to their cultural context.

Yang, M. M. (1994). *Gifts, favors and banquets: The art of social relationships in China.* New York: Cornell University Press.
A detailed account of the working of **guanxi** or 'relationship' in contemporary China.

Internet

Pringle, G. (2004). http://www.cjvlang.com is a delightful site devoted largely to the problems of translating English into Chinese, Vietnamese and Japanese. The focus of this endeavour is Harry Potter. Want to know how Harry Potter comes out in Chinese? Or quidditch, maybe, or a Hungarian Horntail? It's all there. Also an analysis of allusions to classical Chinese poetry in Pink Floyd and other essential information. Includes a Chinese name generator (type in your name and get a Chinese 'translation'), instructions on how to use an abacus and links to other obscurely interesting sites.